HOW TO LIVE WITH A NEUROTIC

HOW TO LIVE
WITH A NEUROTIC

By Albert Ellis

CROWN PUBLISHERS, INC.
NEW YORK, N. Y.

Library of Congress Catalog Card Number: 57-12823

Printed in the United States of America

Fifth Printing, July, 1965

Contents

HOW TO LIVE WITH A NEUROTIC

INTRODUCTION

One of the most frequent questions asked by my patients and acquaintances is: "Tell me, Doctor Ellis, about what percentage of people in our society would you say are neurotic?" I generally reply: "Roughly, about a hundred."

Am I serious about this? Not entirely. From an ideal standpoint, anyone is neurotic who is potentially intelligent and capable but who actually falls below the level of his capabilities and behaves in a needlessly overemotionalized way. In this sense, virtually all of us are more or less disturbed.

From a more practical standpoint, however, psychologists usually label as "neurotic" only those individuals who are so inappropriate in their feelings and so ineffective or disruptive in their behavior that they sooner or later get into rather serious difficulties of their own making. In this sense, I would say (and this, frankly, is a rough guess) that between 20 and 30 per cent of our citizens are neurotic.

This means, if I am correct, that millions of Ameri-

[9]

cans are more or less troubled and many are so disturbed that even the untrained layman can sense their disturbance from their everyday behavior. The question is: What, if anything, can be done? Assuming that you are not too neurotic yourself, and that one of your close relatives or associates is, what can you do to live comfortably with this troubled individual and to try to help him over his difficulties? It is to the answering of this question that the present volume is primarily oriented.

To illustrate what often happens when a relatively well-adjusted person is closely associated with a more seriously disturbed individual, consider the cases of two troubled people who happened to consult me on the same afternoon. The first was a woman of thirty who had been married for six years and whose husband, while not doing anything else outlandish or negative, had given her no money during this time. He paid the rent and food bill, sat at home with her reading the paper on those few nights of the week when he was not at a meeting of one of the numerous organizations to which he belonged, and had intercourse with her about once a month. Otherwise, he did nothing to earn the name of husband. Helping or playing with their two children, taking his wife to a show, telling her about what was happening at the office, discussing with her the latest news—these were all completely foreign to his behavior. Yet when I spoke to this husband, he could see nothing unusual about his marriage, could not understand why his wife was so unhappy, and sincerely believed that theirs was a comfortable, fine relationship.

The second patient was a fifty-year-old man who had been married for twenty-nine years and whose wife, during all this time, had confined herself to their home. She maintained friendly relations only with her mother; had sex relations with her husband about four times a year; and insisted that she was an excellent wife because she never missed cooking a meal or sending her husband's dirty clothes to the laundry. She, like the husband of my first patient, was obviously a seriously disturbed woman who was so fearful of doing anything outside a very simple, rigid routine that she lived on the narrowest possible plane of existence and had no idea about what a good marriage should be.

In both cases the problem was what the normal spouse should do. I explained to both of them, as soon as I realized how disturbed their mates were, that they could do one of three things: seek a divorce or separation; see that their spouses received psychological treatment; or continue to live with their untreated mates and learn to put up with their disturbances.

Usually, in cases like this, the first of the three alternatives is undesirable or impractical, since separation or divorce, especially where children are involved, means heartache and hardship. The second alternative is desirable, but often impossible to achieve, because the disturbed mate will in many or most instances absolutely refuse to accept professional treatment. Consequently, the third alternative—that of living with a neurotic and avoiding being driven to the brink of despair oneself—is the one solution that is both desirable and practical. To help the person who wants to try this third solution, I have developed a technique of teaching which details exactly what has to be done if one is to live successfully with a neurotic. Some of the elements of this teaching are outlined in this book.

For example, I was able to show the thirty-year-old woman that her husband was an exceptionally frightened, insecure person who had been seriously hurt in his relationships with his mother and two previous girl friends, and who consequently was loath to become emotionally involved with anyone else lest he again be rejected and hurt. When his wife understood this, and persisted in giving him all possible warmth and security in spite of his initial coolness, he gradually warmed up, drew considerably closer to her, committed himself to the risks of emotional involvement, and became a more devoted husband.

The case of the fifty-year-old man was not so easy to resolve. His wife proved to be a borderline psychotic who barely maintained her hold on reality by living in a highly restricted fashion. She didn't want to be helped psychotherapeutically; and even consistent kindness

and devotion by her husband were not sufficient to un-
thaw her. He had to be taught, finally, to accept her
as she was and to understand that she was terribly sick
and that her coldness resulted from her sickness rather
than from his behavior. His choice was only twofold:
to separate from his wife, or to accept her *with* her
severe mental illness. Since he did not wish, partly for
religious reasons, to take the first choice, he simply had
—to save his own sanity—to take the second alternative
and become realistically inured to the fact that he was
living with a seriously disturbed woman. This was the
course he was helped to take.

These two cases are typical, not of the problems
which beset individuals living with neurotics or psychotics, but of the choices confronting such individuals.
For assuming that you must, for whatever reasons, live
with a disturbed spouse, relative, friend, or business
associate, you have innumerable bad choices of conduct, but only two or three that are good. Either you
can act in such a manner that your disturbed spouse
or associate becomes less disturbed and easier to live
with; or, if you are not able to help this troubled person, you can become philosophically inured to living
with him in spite of the continuing disturbance. In
some instances, you can use a combination of these two
sensible approaches. The details of how you can live
or work successfully with a neurotic, either by helping
him become less disturbed and/or by learning to take

a rational attitude toward his disturbance, will be given in the later pages of this book.

In trying to show you how to live successfully with a neurotic, this book may also (although this, frankly, is not its main purpose) give you some valuable insights into yourself and your own neurotic trends. For one of the best ways to know yourself is through understanding and helping others.

Take, by way of illustration, another of my cases. A young mother came to see me because she was having serious difficulties with her mother-in-law, who insisted on telling her just how to handle her child, how to treat her husband, and generally how to manage her life. Having felt quite rebellious toward her own mother, and having no intention of acquiring an even more dominant overseer through her marriage, my patient was fighting tooth and nail with her mother-in-law, much to the distress of everyone involved, especially of her husband.

I let her do considerable talking, at first, about her mother-in-law. In the course of her talk it became clear that the mother-in-law was a sweet and well-intentioned but terribly anxious person who could not, in her own life, make even the tiniest decision for fear of making a horrible mistake. She therefore unconsciously kept trying to make other people's (including her daughter-in-law's) decisions for them. She could easily evade any responsibility or blame if, somehow, these decisions turned out to be the wrong ones, since is was not she who had *actually* made them.

My patient soon began to see that what she previously had been considering her mother-in-law's strength and over-decisiveness was actually a mask for this woman's underlying weakness and indecisiveness. Seeing this, she quickly began to lose her antagonism when she was with her mother-in-law; and, instead of resenting the older woman's attempts to boss her around, she now began to pity her and to try to give her more love and security. Relations between the daughter-in-law and her mother-in-law eventually became much more cordial.

One day the patient came to me and quite spontaneously said: "You know, I've been thinking about how my mother-in-law used to act with me and the reasons for her acting as she did. And it occurred to me, when I was telling my oldest daughter how to do her schoolwork the other day, that I have something of my mother-in-law in me, too. After all, I had a bullying mother just as she had, and it's only reasonable to believe that my mother should have had some serious effect on me, too—making me indecisive, that is. And I am! I'm often dreadfully hesitant in doing things.

"And as I heard myself tell my daughter how to do her schoolwork the other day, I suddenly got the picture of my mother-in-law doing exactly the same sort of thing to me. I realized for the first time how alike we are in some ways. That's not a nice thing to contemplate, I'm sure, but it's true, absolutely true.

"Would you believe it—when I saw that, I suddenly stopped, right in the middle (the middle, that is, of telling my daughter about her schoolwork), and I said to myself: 'Now look here—stop bullying that child. You're just trying to get her to be better than you are, to be more decisive than you. But that's not the way. That's an avoidance, instead of a facing, of your own problems. Let the child alone! You're being just as bad as your mother-in-law was!' And I did stop right there, and told her she could do the work any way she liked, as long as it satisfied her. I felt much better after that."

Understanding others, then, is often an open road to understanding oneself. And understanding neurotics is half the battle in understanding one's own neurotic trends. If we live, as we seem to live, in an age and a culture in which emotional disturbance is widespread, we cannot afford to ignore the fact that we ourselves, as part of that age and culture, must be to some degree disturbed. And even if we are not seriously so, it is inevitable that we must go through this life encountering severely troubled people and often becoming more or less involved with them.

Can we recognize, understand, and help some of the emotionally perplexed people with whom we must keep on associating? It is the fundamental premise of this book that we can.

1

THE POSSIBILITY OF HELPING TROUBLED PEOPLE

The most important requirement for living success-fully with, and being of help to, emotionally disturbed individuals is the concept that they *can* be helped. And they can. For human neurosis, as we shall later show in more detail, is distinctly a learned reaction; and anything that is learned can normally be unlearned.

The only thing that makes neurotics hopeless, in other words, is the *belief* that they are hopeless. This is one of the most distinctive, and, one might say, most human, characteristics of men and women: that what they *believe* to be true they usually *make* true; what they *think* is changeless *becomes* so. But if humans believe they can change, they invariably can put this belief into action. And if you believe that you can help them change, your chances of actually doing so are excellent.

I once saw an outstanding lawyer. After twenty-five years of marriage, he had still not learned to satisfy his wife sexually, and when I suggested some obvious methods of doing so, he immediately objected: "But how can I change my sex habits, Dr. Ellis, after having them so long?"

"You," I responded, "are a good trial lawyer, are you not?"

"Yes, I think so."

"And every time you get a new case, you carefully plan it in advance, do you not, in accordance with your past experience with this kind of case, with the judge and jury you are to appear before, and so on?"

"Yes, surely."

"Well," I said, "suppose, after working on one of your cases for a while, you discover that for one reason or another your planned strategy is not effective and seems to be leading to failure. What do you do about it—stick to it nonetheless, because you originally outlined it that way?"

"Why, of course not. I immediately set about planning a new strategy, making another effort."

"Why, then, don't you do the same thing about your relations with your wife? Your old strategy hasn't worked for twenty-five years now. What are you going to do—use it for another twenty-five years before you're convinced that it's hopeless?"

"I never thought about it that way. No, I never gave it a thought."

"Well, don't you believe it's about time you did think about it that way—assuming that your relations with your wife mean at least as much to you as winning a court case?"

P.S.: He did start to think about his relations with his wife, and soon had worked out a much better adjustment.

The point, then, is: emotionally disturbed people are hopeless just as long as they think they are hopeless, and as long as they make no effort to change. For change, virtually by definition, requires effort; and effort usually requires a goal, an idea, a concept. It is the *concept*, therefore, that things can be better than they are—that they *can* be changed—that is the very essence of change itself. It is the concept of hope that negates hopelessness.

Applied to the neurotic relative, friend, or associate with whom you may have steady contact, this means that if you have a concept that he (or she) may change, an idea that he (or she) is not hopelessly disturbed, you will probably be halfway along the path of helping and living successfully with him. It is this concept which, as a practicing psychotherapist, I have spent the last several years giving to my patients who are intimately associated with troubled people.

Consider in this connection one man who consulted me because, while he was finishing his work in graduate school, his exceptionally neurotic wife seemed to be jealous of his school activities and interfered with them in various ways. As soon as he settled down with his books, she would stop her knitting or television-viewing, and start talking to him about irrelevant, unimportant things. When he complained that he just had to do the schoolwork, she said that he acted as if the work were more important than she, that he never spent any time with her and just didn't love her any more. This generally led to a lengthy argument, and by the time they had calmed down, it would be near midnight and his scholastic tasks would remain undone.

At my urging, the husband tried an entirely different approach. First of all, before he tackled any schoolwork, he spent a period of time being exceptionally nice to his wife, telling her that he loved her, and occasionally making sex advances to her. Secondly, he discussed his school activities with his wife; made an effort to get her interested in them so that she would know exactly what was going on, and be as concerned about them as he was himself. He would tell her, especially, about his difficulties with this professor or that instructor, and ask her how she thought he should handle these situations. She soon began to respond to his approach.

Finally, my patient induced his wife to help him with his lessons. He had her do some of his typing, or do some of his arithmetic computations, or read to him when his eyes were tired. In this way, she became vitally interested in the work and began to feel that she was practically going through school with him. After a few weeks of this new approach to the problem, she was entirely co-operative about the school activity and they began to get along together much better. In addition, her own neuroticism became somewhat reduced. She no longer felt so inadequate as she had previously, but began to conceive of herself as making a real contribution to her husband's education, and started to see herself in the same educational class as he.

The same kind of plan can be worked with many neurotic individuals. To try to argue or bully them out of their disturbed behavior is useless and will frequently only make things worse. But if one attempts to discover *why* they act the way they do, and what can be done about getting them to act better, he has an excellent chance of helping them—and, of course, helping himself at the same time. For man is not a completely logical animal; rather, he is a *psycho*logical one. If one treats him in a psychological, understanding way, wonders can be accomplished in some of the seemingly most "hopeless" cases.

Understanding and helping others is largely a matter of one's frame of reference. Most people are so intent on their own problems and worries that they have little time or energy to see things from anyone else's point of view. If you can avoid having a one-sided frame of reference and manage to see things from another's vantage point, you can often be of inestimable help to him.

Relevant in this regard is the case of a patient who was an excellent secretary and normally enjoyed her job. Because she became so upset about some problems that had arisen in her relationship with her husband, however, she began doing quite badly at her work, lost her interest in it, and wanted to quit. Her husband opposed this and pointed out that they needed the money she earned. She tried explaining her feelings to him, but to no avail.

As I frequently do in this type of case, I decided to try to use the husband as an auxiliary therapist, and I asked to see him. He spent most of our first session complaining about his wife's "unreasonable" desire to quit work. He thought that she was doing an excellent job for her employer and that she would be much happier working than not working. He couldn't understand why she was unable to see this.

I carefully explained to him that, theoretically, he was absolutely right. If his wife left her job, she would not only hate herself for running away while the going was rough, but would also be without the ego-support that the job had given her for several years and would therefore tend to act more ineffectively in other respects, such as her housework. This would make her feel even more self-hatred, and a vicious circle would be created.

The husband was gratified to hear that I agreed with his analysis of the situation. He positively beamed, and indicated that he would now go home and belabor his wife with my words and thereby get her to do things his way. I could clearly see him loading his shotgun with the verbal ammunition I had just supplied.

"You're quite right," I said. "But let's look at the thing another way for a moment. Your wife, by wanting to quit work, is acting most illogically, and against her own best interest. But is that the way *she* sees things? Does she not, rather, feel that just because she is now doing poorly on the job, she will lower her self-esteem by remaining on it, and will thereby perform worse in other respects also? Is this not exactly why she feels *forced* to leave, even though she knows the disadvantages, monetary and otherwise, of doing so?"

Yes, he could see that, he said.

"And let us go one step further," I continued. "Your wife knows that, when she was doing well on her job a while ago, she still was getting into trouble with you— about the housework and things like that—doesn't she?"

"Yes, I guess so."

"And now that she's contemplating leaving work, she knows that you are unhappy about this?"

"Yes."

"Well, if—to her way of looking at things—doing a good job doesn't satisfy you and brings her little of the reward she really wants—your love and consideration —why should she keep rewarding you for what to her is nothing but being beaten over the head? Why would it not be more logical—seeing things, again, from *her* frame of reference—for her to do something that would upset and punish you for the unjust way that she doubtlessly thinks that you've been treating her?"

"Now that you put it that way, I guess it might be."

"Exactly. What, actually, you've been doing—even though you haven't realized it—is punishing her when she's doing fine (that is, when she's working well on her job) by criticizing her about the housework and other aspects of her behavior. Then, when she's doing poorly and thinking of quitting, you are unconsciously rewarding her by getting upset yourself, and letting her see that you are unhappy. From her point of view, therefore, if she wants to get back at you for what she considers your unfair criticism, what is the most logical thing for her to do?"

"Just what she's doing now, I guess—punish me by wanting to quit her job."

"Right. She's really not so crazy as it would appear, then, is she?"

"I should say not!"

By showing this husband how to understand and see

things from his wife's frame of reference, I was able to get him to be much less critical of her. He stopped making an issue of her every fault and inadequacy. He minimized the importance of some things she did, pretended not to notice others, and generally employed a more constructive approach. Sensing her husband's changed attitude, the wife began rewarding him—and herself—by doing much better at her work, and soon there was no longer any question of her leaving her job.

In this instance, a distinctly neurotic, illogically thinking woman was enabled to remove some of the pressure she was putting on herself by first having her husband remove *his* pressure on her. When he began to see her actions in *her* frame of reference and to treat her with understanding, she was able to recognize her own distortions of reality and to do something about them. When her husband accepted her as a wife and a human being, she was able to accept herself as an effective secretary as well.

I repeat, therefore: Neurotics can be helped to see things differently themselves, and hence to change their disturbed behavior. And they can also be helped to change when others learn to see them in a different light and to give them leeway to move along less neurotic pathways.

Sometimes still more direct methods may be employed to help emotionally perturbed people solve their problems. A mother once came to see me because her twenty-one-year old daughter was afraid to be left alone in the house and would insist that one or both of her parents remain with her when she had to be home. I tried to have the daughter start a series of psychotherapeutic sessions but she refused to come in for even the first one. By sheer necessity, therefore, I had to work through the mother, who served as an auxiliary therapist.

I asked the mother, in this case, to try a planned method of deconditioning the daughter's fears of remaining alone. I got her to start visiting a nearby neighbor for a few minutes, and then deliberately stay somewhat longer. She would call from the neighbor's, from time to time, and tell the daughter that for some reason she would be delayed a few minutes longer. Gradually, she built up the time of staying away from ten to twenty minutes, and then increased it to thirty and forty minutes.

Every time the mother stayed away for any length of time, she would remark (on my instructions) as soon as she got in: "I'm sorry Mrs. So-and-So detained me, but you know how difficult it is to get away from her. Anyway, you seem to have done fine in my absence. Why, I've actually been gone thirty minutes, and you've done beautifully. I always knew you could and I'm sure that you're not *really* so afraid to be alone." Eventually, after continuing to lengthen her visits over a period of several months, her daughter got more and more used to being alone in the house, and gradually got over her fears.

There are more ways than one, then, of helping a neurotic. None of them is particularly easy; some are quite difficult. But if you take the time and trouble to apply them, they will work—and often work better than your wildest expectations could lead you to believe. Not that miracles can be expected in this connection, although "miracle" is the exact word that is often needed to describe what happens to an emotionally disturbed person when a properly coached member of the family helps solve his problems.

Said one of my patients the other day: "I can't thank you for what you've done for us, for me and my family, Doctor. It's really a miracle."

I replied: "It's not what *I've* done, but what *you've* done for yourself and your family that's accomplished this 'miracle.' I, as I told you during our very first session, can merely help you understand things, can point out ways in which you can aid yourself. But *you've* got to do them, act on them. I can't do anything for you; you can work—and have worked—beautifully to help yourself. You really have only yourself to thank."

What this woman had done was to accept her nineteen-year-old daughter's harsh verbal attacks, which had continued to occur for almost ten years. Instead of getting perturbed about them as she had done for a long time before coming to see me, she had begun to understand how and why they arose, and consistently to meet them with quietness, calmness, kindness. The result, within six weeks, was amazing: the daughter had not only stopped berating the mother, but had become co-operative and loving, had suddenly stopped spending all her time in the college library, and had begun dating boys. A real "miracle." And yet, only a little understanding, a changed maternal attitude, had been involved. Nothing but that—and a nineteen-year-old girl who had previously been almost certainly doomed to an unhappy, self-hating, emotionally-ill existence was now being given a more than even chance to develop into a well-adjusted human being.

Can virtually anyone help almost anyone else to overcome emotional quirks and upsets? No, not exactly. For the would-be helper, aside from having good intentions and real patience, must himself be not too disturbed to begin with; and the same may be said of the one to be helped. Individuals who are deeply disturbed should normally be seen by psychologists and psychiatrists; and those who would help them should obtain psychological consultation. Otherwise, serious harm may result.

This means, specifically, that you should not try to cure your friends or relatives who are exceptionally depressed, who think very little of themselves, who are unusually agitated, or who are behaving in a clearly bizarre manner. Such individuals may be overtly or underlyingly psychotic and may require immediate professional care (and sometimes institutionalization). By all means, leave these deeply disturbed associates to those who are psychiatrically trained.

The fact remains, however, that many of our fellow citizens are not so severely disturbed that they must have professional psychological or psychiatric care— even though almost all of them might well benefit from at least a few consultations. And the fact also remains that many who actually should have intensive psychotherapy, for one reason or another, simply won't. It is these who can often be helped considerably by the wise intercession of a friend or relative who is willing to take the time and trouble to understand them and to assist in guiding them through their perplexity.

Instructive in this connection is the case of a mother who came to see me to complain that her twenty-nine-year-old unmarried daughter was not really trying to acquire a husband. The girl went on dates with boys but somehow didn't go with the marrying kind; and whenever the mother pointedly brought this fact to her attention, the daughter would argue and scream like a fishwife and tell the mother to mind her own business. What, the mother asked, could she do with a child like that?

I, too, tried to get the mother to mind her own business. I attempted to show her that, if her daughter was not marrying, it probably was because she hadn't sufficient confidence in herself to try to find the right kind of man; or that she was so disturbed by her mother's incessant proddings that she consciously or unconsciously derived satisfaction from spiting the mother by not marrying. Anyway, I said, the girl was twenty-nine years old, and what she did or did not do about marriage was clearly her own affair. The less the mother nagged her, the more likely she was to get married.

The mother couldn't see this at all, and thought that I was somehow in league with her daughter (and the devil) to keep the girl unmarried. I saw that I wasn't going to get anywhere with the mother, since she wouldn't admit that she might in any way be contributing to the problem, and kept insisting that her daughter was unbalanced and ungrateful, and so I asked her to send the daughter to see me. I was, frankly, not thinking so much of working with the daughter—though it was probable that she would need help, too—but of seeing whether I could induce her to assist me with the mother's problem.

When the daughter came to see me, I realized immediately that she was a disturbed girl. But she was willing to acknowledge that she had problems and said she would like to do something about trying to solve them. After several visits, she developed insight into her own behavior and began to see, as I had guessed from my first talk with the mother, that she was concerned about being prodded into marrying, and that unconsciously she was resisting by continually selecting unmarriageable boy friends. Putting this insight to good use, she started to be more selective in her choice of steady dates and to work toward a good relationship with one boy in particular.

In the meantime, even before she changed her dating pattern, I got this girl to work with me on the mother's problem. After I explained to her how disturbed her mother was, and what some of the reasons probably were, the daughter stopped arguing with her mother and, at my suggestion, calmly accepted almost everything she said. Realizing her mother's overanxiety, she would usually tell just what her mother wanted to hear about the boys with whom she, the daughter, was going out. Whatever her mother said, no matter how outlandish or provocative, she calmly went—or at least seemed to go—along with (even though, in practice, she often completely ignored her mother's views.

The mother was so impressed with the daughter's changed attitudes, and especially with her new-found calmness, that she herself found nothing negative to respond to, and she began to calm down. She came to see me several weeks after she had first appeared, was quite apologetic for her previous antagonism toward me, and said that she was most gratified at the changes I had wrought in her daughter, who had become "a completely different girl."

Actually, the daughter was not that much changed, although she had begun to tackle her own basic problems and eventually (some six months later) was on the way to solving them. The mother, ironically, was considerably improved herself. Her daughter's example of calm, reasonable behavior had taken away much of her own excuse for irrationality. Where I, as psychotherapist, had signally failed to make any inroads on the mother's neurosis, the daughter's insight and actions had helped enormously.

My intimate association with many cases like the ones related in this chapter thoroughly convinces me that, with the proper knowledge and effort, almost any nonprofessional person who is himself not too seriously troubled can help one of his close relatives, friends, or associates who is more deeply disturbed. Of course the helper must understand what a neurotic is, the probable causes of neurosis, and some of the methods that can help change neurotic behavior patterns. With this knowledge, and a strong determination to apply it in practice, a helper can often achieve remarkable results.

What, then, is and what makes a human being a neurotic? Let us see.

2

HOW TO RECOGNIZE AN EMOTIONALLY DISTURBED PERSON

What is a neurotic?

Basically, an individual who consistently acts illogically, irrationally, inappropriately, and childishly. Although theoretically he is able to think for himself and plan his days for effective, happy living, he actually falls back on unintelligent behavior, failing to attain some of his own dearest goals and sabotaging his own best potentialities.

Is it, then, easy to recognize a neurotic when you meet one?

Not necessarily. For there are many *truly* stupid people around. These individuals, because of inherited or early-acquired mental defects, simply cannot think clearly, act grown-up, do things effectively. They just are not bright enough to plan and execute rational modes of living. Not knowing enough to come in out of the rain, they frequently get soaking wet. But because there is a definite physical (neurological) reason for their nonrational, childish behavior, it is inaccurate to label them "neurotic."

Neurosis, moreover, should not be confused with mere unhappiness. Some people—millions, in fact— are *appropriately* unhappy. Take, for instance, those who do not have enough to eat, or who are not bright enough to get good jobs, or who are chronically ill. How could they be very happy?

Neurotics, then, are individuals who are unreasonably and unnecessarily bothered or bewildered. They are *more* unhappy, or inefficient, or fearful than they, theoretically, need be. A great many of them have more than enough wherewithal—good looks, high intelligence, fine talents—to get along successfully in this world. But somehow they don't. That "somehow," that "something," which comes between their potential abilities and their actual achievements—*that* is their neurosis.

One of the fundamental reasons it is not always easy to say who is and who is not emotionally disturbed is that neurotics are great cover-uppers. The last thing they want known is how illogical, how neurotic they are. They often resort to all kinds of subterfuges and defenses to prevent recognition of their true emotional colors. They compartmentalize, for instance, and hold their neuroses to one or two major aspects of their lives, while acting with reasonable normality in most other respects. Or they compensate and do a splendid job in one area—such as in their business dealings, for example—while virtually falling apart in other respects. Or they go through silly rituals and magical devotions within the confines of their own homes but act convincingly sane on the outside.

Many neurotics, consequently, seem perfectly happy and effective to some of their closest associates, even though the line separating them from serious disturbance is pitiably thin.

Another obstacle in the way of recognizing neurotic symptoms is their infinite variety. All neurotics, to be sure, tend to be peculiar—to some degree, irrational and "crazy." But the roads to emotional perplexity are confusingly multiple. Where one neurotic has terrible fears of doing almost anything, another shows his disturbance by needlessly risking his neck every day in some dangerous enterprise. While one lies abed all day and refuses to do any work, another frantically consumes himself in a dozen violent endeavors. One disturbed woman hypochondriacally insists that she is wasting away from a score of imaginary ills; and another with a cancerous ovary insists that she is not sick, that there is no death, and that her Yoga breathing exercises will take care of all her ills.

A further problem in differentiating neurosis from other forms of irregular human behavior is the fact that eccentricity and neurosis are by no means necessarily the same. Virtually all neurotics are, in one way or another, eccentric; but all eccentrics are not neurotic. If a Henry David Thoreau, for example, wants to desert Concord society for a while to live in the Walden woods, or if a Mahatma Gandhi wishes to lead a movement of passive resistance against the British, these eccentricities and heresies do not necessarily constitute proof of emotional aberration. Rebels and saints are occasionally crazed; but not always.

It is possible—though not easy—to disagree profoundly with the great majority of one's fellows and yet, in one's own life goals and ideals, be perfectly consistent. Neurosis is an *inner* contradiction, a discord between what the individual wants to do for himself and the means he uses to achieve his own goals. Eccentricity may merely be a contradiction between an individual's ideals and those of his neighbors. It does not *have* to be a symptom of emotional disturbance, although it often is.

How, then, in view of some of the possibly confusing evidence and of our inability to see inner contradictions and unconscious conflicts, can we tell a neurotic from a so-called normal or well-adjusted individual?

Mainly, by recognizing his most important neurotic manifestations or symptoms. Some of the main symptoms of emotional disturbance are these:

Indecision, doubt, and conflict. Neurotics are often indecisive, hesitant, doubtful. They want to be or to do one thing but are afraid to make a mistake, to fail in their own and others' eyes. So they waver, decline to make decisions, refuse to commit themselves or to take full responsibility for anything.

One neurotic girl I knew left her husband to live with another man, but then kept finding fault with her lover because he lacked some of the characteristics of the husband. She wavered between the two, and literally shuttled back and forth between them several times, before she finally was able to see that it was not *their* traits but her *own* indecisiveness which constituted the real issue. When she faced this fact, and started to work seriously on her own problems, she had no trouble in making up her mind—in this instance in favor of the husband.

Fear and anxiety. Virtually all neurotics are irrationally afraid of something. On the surface, they may be the fearless, mountain-climbing type. Underneath, they are jelly. In the last analysis, they are afraid of what people think, of doing the wrong thing, of not having others love and approve of them. Sometimes they honestly know and admit this. But more often, they translate their fears of social and self-disapproval into more concrete phobias, such as the fear of walking on the street, or of being cooped up at home. Look beneath a neurotic's defenses and you will invariably find an irrational dread.

What are neurotics afraid of? Everything imaginable. I have seen strong, hulky brutes of men, typical football-player types, who quailed at the sight of a small bug; or who simply could not ride on subway trains; or who broke into a sweat at the mere idea of going to a party; or who could not go through with a job interview if their lives depended on it. I have seen women who bore five children without flinching or who uncomplainingly had extensive dental work done, but who would go into an extreme state of panic at the contemplation of exchanging an article in a store, or being examined by a physician, or eating a banana, or giving a bridge party. And even among those who are physically brave, there are many neurotics who are terribly afraid of what others may say or think.

Inadequacy feelings. Emotionally disturbed people usually feel that they are inadequate, worthless, wicked in general or specific ways. They think that they should be this and are only that; or should be that and are, alas, only this. They do not merely recognize their own faults; they inordinately magnify, catastrophize, them. And, above all, they think it is *wrong* for them to have any failing; they *blame* themselves incessantly for having them.

One of the worst cases of this kind that I have ever seen was that of a woman whose husband was blatantly unfaithful to her and would regale her with stories of how many other women he saw and what he did with them. When, driven to distraction, she sought the sympathetic ear of one of her male cousins, and started to become attached to him because of his kindness, she began to feel terribly guilty, began to look upon herself as the vilest kind of adulteress, and thought that she was not a fit mother for her children. I had a difficult time showing her that it was not her current behavior but her long-standing and deep-seated feelings of worthlessness which truly underlay her ceaseless self-criticism.

Guilt and self-blame. Troubled people, like the girl just described, are usually severe moralists. They blame others and themselves for innumerable desires and deeds. As Freud emphasized, they have particular difficulty in accepting their own sex drives. But this is less than half of it, for they also condemn themselves for many nonsexual things they do. They tend to be too conscientious in their thoughts and too lax in their actions. They know what they should do—and don't do it. Then they berate themselves unmercifully.

One of my patients who had the highest standards of personal conduct and honesty obtained a job doing door-to-door selling of encyclopedias. He liked the work because he felt that he was helping raise the cultural level of the families to whom he sold, and he

began to do very well at the job. After a while, however, he became so disturbed about the possibility of
making the slightest exaggerated claim for his product
that he spent hours and hours rewording his memor-
ized sales talk. Even that did not satisfy him, and he
began to add to the talk all kinds of qualifications and
hedgings, so that his customers began to feel that he
was apologizing for even trying to sell them the books.
Naturally his sales fell off and, in sheer desperation, he
was driven to seek psychotherapy. He was finally helped
when he began to see that his phobia against telling
any kind of exaggerated story or half-truth stemmed
from his mother's great fear that he would follow in
his father's footsteps and become a cardsharp.

Supersensitivity and oversuspiciousness. Emotionally
disturbed individuals are often supersensitive and over-
suspicious. They do not merely believe that others dislike them; they look for, actively ferret out, seek until
they ultimately find, this dislike. They are so underlyingly guilty about their own behavior that they become convinced everyone else sees them through their
own distorted vision and, consequently, detests them.

A clear example was provided by one of my deeply
disturbed patients who noticed that I sometimes put
my two fingers over my upper lip and hold them
against the under part of my nose. This I do indis-
criminately, with patients, friends, intimates. Said this
particular girl: "I notice that you hold your fingers

over your nose. This is because you think I smell bad, isn't it?" "No," I replied, "but obviously *you* think that I (and everyone else) thinks you smell bad." "How did you know?" she asked.

Hostility and resentment. Many neurotics are hostile and aggressive. Hating themselves, they tend to hate others. Feeling that the world is doing them in, they want to retaliate in kind. Being frustrated, largely by their own irrational behavior, they often respond with the common sequel of frustration—aggression against the presumably frustrating society and the people in it.

The treasurer of a group to which I once belonged kept getting into difficulties with the other officers of the group because he insisted on doing things in a high-handed, unorthodox manner. When the others complained about his methods he was most aggrieved, and viewed the other men as unfair spoilers of his projects. As a result of his frustration—or, actually, of his telling himself that he *should* not be frustrated—he became hostile not only to his fellow officers, but to almost everyone and everything else. If given the chance, he would complain for hours at a time about politicians, bureacrats, modern fiction, mothers-in-law, school systems, and a dozen other pet annoyances. He could never see that he had little reason for his hostility other than the fact that he disliked interference from others, and always wanted to do things in his own peculiar way.

Ingratiation. Many troubled people spinelessly curry favor with others at the expense of their own self-respect. In an effort to win love and approval, they slavishly bow to their relatives and associates, abase themselves—and then hate themselves more and feel greater insecurity and rejection. Moreover, because they loathe their own ingratiating tendencies, they frequently try to compensate by reversing themselves and becoming hostile toward those whose favor they seek.

A typical neurotic pattern is that of one of my own acquaintances, who will apologize to his wife for everything he does or does not do; then he will verbally slice her to ribbons for something trivial she has done, such as forgetting to pick up the laundry. Similarly, one of my patients encourages all her friends to use her as a doormat. Then she complains to me for hours about how nasty her father is. When I point out to such people that there may be a significant connection between how they bow down to others and how they hate these others, they often find it difficult to see how the first of these attitudes could lead to the second. But once they do see the connection and give up their ingratiating behavior, it is remarkable how quickly a large part of their hostility vanishes.

Inefficiency and stupidity. Neurotics, even when they are great achievers, are often inefficient. Many do things badly or not at all. Others do too much or achieve success the too-hard way—with a needless sacrifice of time, nervous and physical energy, and pleasure. They work unsystematically, without proper planning, or work compulsively, with involved systems that bog them down and promote complications. They are so emotionally blocked that they will not or cannot think their problems through logically. Or they think them through rationally enough and then continue acting in the same irrational manner as before.

I treated a very brilliant girl who was majoring in philosophy and doing exceptionally well. One day she came to me and said that her parents were away from home and she was so sloppy at keeping house that she was afraid that she would soon be invaded by rats. "Why don't you clean the place?" I asked.

"Oh, but it's such lovely weather," she replied, "that I'd rather sit in the sun and enjoy myself."

"But you're not weighing up the whole equation," I said. "You're not thinking logically."

"What do you mean?"

"Well, you're equating doing the housework, on the one hand, with sitting in the sun and enjoying yourself, on the other hand. Naturally, in terms of that equation, you'll continue to sit in the sun. But the real equation is: doing the housework, on the one side—*and* liking yourself; or sitting in the sun, on the other side—*and* loathing yourself."

"Yes, I guess that's right."

"Now which side adds up to the most enjoyment?"

"I see."

She promptly began cleaning the house.

Self-deceit and lack of realism. Virtually all neurotics lie to themselves and refuse to accept reality the way it is. Instead of squarely facing their frustrations, admitting their failings, or unwhiningly accepting the grim facts of life, they tend to rationalize, evade issues, blame others, and generally construct a picture of the world that is more poetry than truth.

A physician whom I had known from college days continued to visit me every few years, and almost every time he arrived he would have in tow a good-looking female companion who obviously had nothing in common with him intellectually. He would take me aside during the course of the evening and longwindedly explain what a fine person she was, what her sexual advantages were, and how in many ways she was much more desirable than girls of his own cultural and intellectual background. I would quietly ask a few pointed questions to indicate my scepticism about his achieving a lasting relationship with the girl; but he would defend his choice spiritedly. Then, on his next visit, he would tell me how right I had been about the last girl; but *this* girl, now—and he would launch into a highly unrealistic evaluation of his current companion.

It was not until a good many years had passed, and my friend had finally had some intensive psychotherapy, that he felt free to admit that the whole series of pretty girls had been the result of his underlying deep-seated feelings of inadequacy in the presence of bright and substantial women. These inadequacy feelings had led him, via the common route of wishful thinking, into unrealistically assessing his girl friends and deceiving himself into believing that they were remarkable women.

Defensiveness. Once they begin lying to themselves, neurotics have to set up a system of defense against being unmasked and having to face unpleasant realities. Usually, they devise an elaborate network of devious reactions, and consciously pretend that they are feeling or acting one way when they are unconsciously motivated by quite different feelings. Some of the common forms of neurotic defensiveness are these:

• Rationalization—providing a reason for the commission of an act one considers blameworthy. Examples: the mother who has a neurotic need to criticize her son, but insists that she does so only for his good; the man who collects pornographic literature and insists that he does so only because he is scientifically interested in sex.

• Compensation—acting well in one area to set up an unconscious smoke screen for neurotically running away from another dangerous area. Examples: the girl who is afraid to go to dances, but practically lives in the public library instead and becomes an authority on medieval history; the man who becomes a great base-ball manager because he is afraid that as a player he would not excel.

• Identification—compensating for one's own weakness by becoming closely allied with someone who appears to be strong. Examples: the physical coward who feels that he is a real man because he associates with bullies and bruisers; the homely teen-age girl who feels at one with her favorite female movie star and refuses to face her own problems.

• Projection—throwing the blame or responsibility for one's own failings onto others. Example: a man who hates his father accuses the father of hating him; or incorrectly views other men as hating their fathers.

• Repression—unconsciously forgetting about aspects of one's own behavior of which one is ashamed or which one looks upon as painful. Examples: the girl who cannot remember anything about the night she lost her virginity; the fellow who remembers only the tennis games he won and conveniently forgets those he lost.

• Resistance—refusing to face unpleasant facts about oneself, even when they are pointedly brought to one's attention. Examples: the psychotherapy patient who refuses to admit that he has hostile feelings toward his mother although his therapist *shows* him that his relations with her have clearly followed a hostile pattern; the poor card-player who insists that he is playing well even when his many mistakes are pointed out to him.

• Transference—unconsciously displaying toward a person or a group attitudes which are not based on reality, but on the fact that the person or group has some traits in common with individuals, especially one's parents, who may have been significant in one's past. Examples: the teen-ager who, because he resents his parents, may be rebellious against teachers, policemen, and other authority figures; the man who resents his second wife because she has a few traits in common with his mother and his first wife.

• Grandiosity—unconsciously overcompensating by seeing oneself as much better than one actually is because one fears, underneath, that he is inadequate. Examples: the revolutionist who, in order to be kingpin, sets up a group of his own which actually differs little from the group from which he has broken off; the man who, although he is an alcoholic derelict, thinks that the world owes him a living because he is really superior to others.

• Reaction formation—refusing to acknowledge feelings (such as fear or hostility) which one does not want to face, but unconsciously expressing the reverse emotion. Examples: the mother who really loathes her son, but smothers him with affection and insists she adores him; the fellow who is insanely jealous of his friend's prowess, but refuses to admit this to himself or others and, instead, becomes this friend's best press agent.

• Refusal to perform—avoiding or postponing a performance or test where one is afraid of failing, and telling oneself that he would succeed if he did buckle down to it. Example: the college student who puts off doing his work till the end of the term, takes his exams without having had time to catch up with the work, and then tells himself that if he had worked harder he would have done better on the exams.

All these are typical defense mechanisms which the neurotic unconsciously may resort to because consciously he does not want to face the fact that he is not doing as well as he would like to do.

Rigidity and compulsiveness. Neurotics feel unsafe, insecure. In an effort to attain a greater degree of security, they frequently adopt an arbitrary set of rules and stick to them rigidly. Because they are always afraid of doing the wrong thing, or letting their thoughts and deeds get beyond their control, they tend to pick certain aspects of life which they *can* easily control and then stick compulsively to these straight and narrow paths. They often devise magical rituals and formulas —such as going through a studied routine before bedtime—to give themselves a feeling that some unknown power is protecting them as long as they stick closely to their chosen formulas.

One of the college students I was treating always took six sharply-pointed pencils into every examination and lined them up neatly in front of her. Then she proceeded to ignore them entirely and to use a ball-point pen for the exam. The pencils gave her a feeling of reserve strength—in case something happened to her pen. More importantly, they served to make her feel that if she temporarily forgot anything that she had studied for the exam, the information was really still stored in her mind and could be recalled, just as the pencils could be used in case something happened to her pen. After she had achieved more confidence in herself, as a result of several psychotherapeutic sessions, she was able to take her exams without the compulsively-arranged extra pencils, for she was now able to rely on her general ability rather than on a special ritual.

Shyness and withdrawal. Believing that they may easily do the wrong thing and that others will spot their mistakes, numberless neurotics become shy and withdrawn, and retreat into various kinds of solitude. Constructively, they may follow useful occupations which demand solitude, such as working alone in a laboratory or being a forest ranger. Destructively, they may merely avoid people, stay alone in their rooms, or literally become hermits. In that way they find themselves in one of the frequent neurotic vicious circles: because they are afraid of people they withdraw from society—and thus become more afraid of people.

An extreme case was that of a twenty-two-year-old boy who had immense difficulty getting himself up in the morning. When he finally did start for work, he would stand in a corner in the end compartment of the train and face the side of the compartment so that others could not see him. He took his lunch to work and remained alone in his office to eat it. When he returned home at night, he ate quickly and then went right to bed. He was so shy that he literally could never look other people in the eye. When at last he managed to do this without blushing and quickly averting his gaze, he was as happy as anyone else would have been at making a varsity football team or winning Phi Beta Kappa honors.

Antisocial or psychopathic behavior. Many neurotics take a rebellious path from the start, and try to compensate for their underlying feelings of inadequacy by becoming "tough guys" or cynics. A few of these go to real extremes and become unregenerate juvenile delinquents or adult criminals. Although some psychologists view these so-called psychopaths as special kinds of warped personalities, my own experience with scores of them convinces me that, at bottom, their "psychopathy" is a defensive covering used by these confused, frightened, self-blaming individuals to harden themselves against underlying feelings of rejection, self-pity, and deep-seated supersensitivity. Relatively few neurotics are "psychopaths"; but dig beneath so-called psychopathic behavior and you invariably find a neurotic (or psychotic) underpinning.

When I was Chief Psychologist of the New Jersey Department of Institutions and Agencies, I interviewed a young man who had a long series of delinquencies on his record, including burglary, holdups, and stolen cars. At the time I saw him he had just been apprehended for shooting his girl friend, crippling her for life, because he was jealous of her wearing sweaters which revealed her buxom figure to other males. He was not the slightest bit remorseful about this act, nor about any of the criminal acts which he had previously perpetrated. All told, he was one of the coolest customers I had ever interviewed.

In the course of the interview I asked this young desperado a few routine questions about his sex history, including any oral genital relations with females in which he may have indulged. "Whadya mean by asking me questions like that?" he bellicosely interrupted. "Whadya think I am, anyway?"

"You mean," I asked, "that you think such things are wrong?"

"Wrong! I should say so! Besides, whadya think the other guys would say about me if I did things like that? I'd never be able to face them."

Behind even the hardest "psychopathic" mien, then, it is not too difficult to find neurotic supersensitivity.

Psychosomatic symptoms and hypochondria. Not all physical ailments are caused by neurosis, but many have a neurotic component. Emotionally disturbed people sometimes worry themselves into sickness by keeping their muscles and nervous systems in a continual state of excitement and tension, thus helping to bring on such psychosomatic complaints as ulcers, high blood pressure, asthma and heart palpitations. Moreover, when they become afflicted with a physical ailment, they commonly do everything possible to prolong and aggravate it and to use it as an excuse for their emotional upsets. Neurotics do not always create physical illnesses, but they do encourage and use them.

One of my many hypochondriacal patients complained that he just could not stop worrying about the possibility of serious illness. If he had a pain in his head, he was sure it was a brain tumor. A simple cough convinced him immediately that he was tuberculous. A stomach twinge set him quickly to thinking of cancer. And whatever he thought he had, he was positive that it would be fatal.

"Why do you keep worrying about these illnesses all the time?" I asked.

"Well, think how terrible it would be if I died— and at my young age, too, before I've barely lived."

"Maybe so," I said. "But did it ever occur to you that you're spending so much time and energy worrying over the possibility of dying young that you're actually giving yourself no opportunity to enjoy the life you're now living? Under these circumstances, what have you to live for, anyway?"

"Not very much, you make it appear."

"You mean," I said, "*you* make it appear. *You're* the one who's wrecking your own life by worrying over something that is almost entirely beyond your control."

"I never thought of it that way," said the patient. "Maybe you've got something there." And, shortly thereafter, he began to think more and worry less.

Crackpot-ism and bizarreness. Not all eccentrics, as we previously noted, are necessarily neurotic, but plenty of them are. Not being able to get along too well in this world, they frequently try to create a world of their own and consequently acquire all kinds of crackpot, bizarre notions about how to live.

When neurotics become sufficiently bizarre to lose sight of reality entirely, we call them psychotics. Neuroticism may be deemed a reasonably mild evasion of reality; psychosis is an extreme form of escape from the real world into one of illusion or fantasy. Psychotics generally have an even lower estimate of themselves than do neurotics, and consequently the defenses they erect against accepting themselves as they are, are more dramatic than neurotic defenses, often consisting of hallucinations, extreme projections, godlike feelings, and the like. Or else they over-accept their "faults," continually berate themselves, and become exceptionally depressed.

Neurotics, as well as psychotics, may engage in bizarre behavior, and therefore such behavior is not necessarily to be looked upon as a signal for carting an individual off to the nearest mental hospital. The superintendent of the apartment house where I once lived kept inventing schemes for winning at the race track. Essentially, his system consisted of doubling his previous bets and keeping on doubling until finally a winner came up. He was quite intelligent and had considerable experience with racing, and so he was well aware that any such scheme as this could only be practical when it was backed by virtually unlimited funds. With very limited resources at his disposal, however, he insisted upon trying out one new scheme after another, and of course he lost heavily. But his desire to make a killing, to prove his genius to the world and thereby magically erase his tremendous underlying feeling of worthlessness was so great that he continued to devise bizarre, sure-fire betting systems.

Unhappiness and depression. A few emotionally troubled people manage to compensate well for their inner insecurities and remain outwardly content. But the average disturbed person is either steadily or sporadically unhappy and depressed. He tends to be filled with self-pity and pessimism. His unhappiness does not, by itself, prove that he is neurotic, but such unhappiness is a frequent by-product of neurosis.

A family friend, a sixty-year-old woman, was as unhappy an individual as I have ever seen. Every time she came to visit, her face was literally lined with sorrow, and she shed copious tears as she described the woeful time she had had during the past few days. Night after night, she reported, she lay awake, sometimes for the entire night, crying, sighing, moaning, verbally bewailing her sorrowful lot. The cause of her despair? The fact that her only living son seemed determined to die a bachelor, thus leaving her with only two female and no male grandchildren. (Her daughter, mother of the two girls, was past childbearing.) Because of this horrible situation, she alleged, her entire purpose in life was negated, and she might just as well never have been born. When I attempted to show her that it could not possibly be this situation itself but, rather, only her unrealistic and childish attitude toward it that was causing her sorrow, she considered me an unfeeling brute who had no understanding of a woman's role in life.

Self-centeredness and inability to love. Most neurotics have an inordinate desire to receive, and an infinitesimal ability to give, love. They are so incessantly concerned with themselves and their own problems that they have neither the time, the energy, nor the inclination truly to care for another human being. Neurotics often fall violently in love; that is, they become obsessed with individuals whom they would like to have love them. But they have little ability to love: to want to help another person achieve his *own* growth and happiness for his *own* ends.

I particularly remember, in this connection, one of the first girls I dated, when I was in my teens. She, because of what I later began to see was acute dissatisfaction with herself, had a tremendous need to be loved, adored, approved, deified. When she met a boy who she believed was the right answer to her need for love, she became quickly, violently, attached to him, and insisted that she loved him passionately. Then, as soon as she discovered that her beloved was not exclusively interested in worshiping her and bolstering her ego, but instead had some deep-seated needs of his own, she took the discovery as an absolute betrayal, insisted that the boy did not "really" or "truly" love her, and broke up the relationship with him in order to start seeking a new great love. This ceaseless, fruitless search for perfect love has continued, as far as I know, to the present day, through several marriages and innumerable affairs. The one thing she has never sought, however, is the answer to the question of why she herself keeps demanding amative perfection.

Tenseness and inability to relax. Because they are so preoccupied with themselves and so constantly worrying about whether they are doing the right or wrong things, disturbed people cannot very well relax. As a result, they suffer from a physical tension which evidences itself in muscular ailments, poor coordination, the inability to sit still, and so on. Sometimes the result is psychological tension during which the disturbed report that they feel emotionally numb, would like to take out their brains and place them in the refrigerator, or are afraid of something but don't even know what they fear. A certain amount of effort is essential to normal living; otherwise we would not succeed in doing anything or getting anywhere. But the neurotic experiences unnecessary effort: strain which he himself causes by his groundless fears, his irrational worries about what other people are thinking about him.

Recently there came to see me a young girl who could only with great difficulty describe her tenseness. She was ashamed that she bit her nails. But, aside from this information, she could hardly tell me how she felt. She would vaguely start a sentence: "I don't know what it is—I can't say how I feel—I just don't know . . ." Then she would hesitate before taking another stab: "I'm not sure—I don't want to do anything. No, that's not it: I don't know what I do want to do. I just don't know exactly how to put it . . ."

Only after considerable questioning could I elicit the fact that she was completely restless. She could stay in her own room for no more than a few moments; did not feel comfortable even when she was talking to her parents; could read for only a few pages; could not, in fact, do anything for more than a very short while without jumping up and wanting to do something else, although not knowing what else she wanted to do.

This girl, then, was exceptionally tense. And the

reasons for her tension were not difficult to trace. Most of the things she wanted to do, such as becoming a champion ice-skater, her parents opposed: thus, either she refrained from doing these things, or she did them with a feeling of guilt. What she did *not* want to do— including going to art school—her parents virtually insisted upon. So either she refused to do these things and was upset because of her parents' censure, or she did them and loathed her parents for their pressuring. The only independence she was able to achieve was by actively rebelling against her family. Inevitably, this situation made her so irritable and indecisive that she could not for a moment relax.

Overexcitability and manic tendencies. Some disturbed people, instead of being depressed, become overexcited or overelated. Trying to compensate for their (conscious or unconscious) feelings of inadequacy, they may become unusually exhibitionistic, overbearing, or life-of-the-party-ish. Other troubled individuals, in order to avoid facing their own disturbances, constantly attempt to keep themselves stimulated by outward forms of excitement; normal conditions of daily life leave them bored and listless.

A prime example of neurotic extraversion is the case of a thirty-six-year-old male who was largely ignored as a child because his parents devoted most of their attention to his highly talented older sister. In consequence, he now cannot bear to be ignored by anyone, or to be merely a member of an audience, or to have others fail to consider him outstanding. While not a manic, he easily becomes surly and depressed. If he does *not* continually impress people, he thinks they will find him inferior. Being enormously self-centered, he is not really interested in other people and has no vital interests aside from showing off. Consequently he strives incessantly for attention—to be the center of some group. If this group is doing something different and unconventional—such as playing strip poker or smoking marijuana—so much the better. He will participate in the attention—and admiration, he believes—that accrues to this group, and he will outstrip and out-smoke the others. "Anything for excitement" is his motto, but what he unconsciously means is anything to divert him from thinking seriously about himself and facing his intense feelings of inferiority.

Inertia and lack of direction. Many neurotics tend to be unenergetic and to lack any definite goals in life. They are, in fact, on a sort of sitdown strike against life, since they believe that the world owes them a living and that they should not be required to work hard or discipline themselves to get the things they want. Deep in their hearts, they do want to strive for something, to realize some goal. But as soon as they meet difficulties in their striving, they give up and withdraw from competition. Once they give up, getting back to work becomes even harder because their inertia makes them poor in accomplishment, which in turn leads to a feeling of hopelessness and more inertia.

One twenty-six-year-old came to see me because he was impotent. We soon discovered that both his father and mother were exceptionally hard-working people who had built up a large commercial enterprise by devoting almost all their working hours to it. He had resented this all his life and felt that the time his parents had put into the business was rightfully his.

Because of his resentment, he hated all work and spent most of his time hanging around poolrooms and bowling alleys. In his sex relations, he also unconsciously refused to "work" at satisfying his partners, and hence became impotent. Only after he was able to begin facing his sitdown strike against employment and against females was he able to get along with his chosen life work (selling) and to become sexually adequate.

Overambitiousness and compulsive striving. Some neurotics compensate for their quarrels with themselves by working themselves practically to death. Not that all hard workers are disturbed people; in fact, well-adjusted individuals usually work harder than the average. But neurotics overwork themselves not for satisfying achievement but because they feel so insecure that they *need* fame or fortune; because in constant activity they can distract themselves from some of the psychological pain that plagues them; because work often gives them an excuse to avoid things of which they are terribly afraid—for example, engaging in love affairs or attending social gatherings.

A woman of my acquaintance achieved real distinction as a writer of historical novels. She was not a happy person, however, and once when I discussed some of her problems with her, she freely admitted that most of her success as a writer had come from very hard work. Where other writers did months of research for a novel, she did years. She spent hour after hour in the library, rewrote her plots and her characterizations again and again, drew involved maps and genealogical tables as she was writing, and generally was so perfectionist in everything she wrote that her readers always marveled at the fineness of her details. And well they might, since these details were wrung, as it were, from her very life's blood.

She admitted to me that, although she had been something of a child prodigy in the field of literature and had had financial and critical success from her teens onward, she had never really done anything for herself, for her own happiness, during all this time. She was always so intent on the highest possible achievement, on getting acclaim for what she did, that taking vacations, going to shows and concerts, and even relaxing at home were almost entirely foreign to her life. She lived only for her work; she herself was a nonentity as a personality.

Escapism and avoidance of responsibility. Instead of

facing and working out their serious difficulties, emotionally disturbed individuals frequently see a problem and run. They refuse to discipline themselves or to assume the normal responsibilities of life. Often they attempt to live as perpetual children, and if they marry, they live as child-wives and child-husbands. If they can literally run away from difficulties, they do so: to a new home, a new job, a new marriage, a new wardrobe. When they cannot actually run, they find numerous ways of refusing to assume life's usual duties and obligations.

One of my most difficult patients was a young man who was a positive genius at avoiding the necessary tasks of life. He never kept a job for more than a few weeks, but left it, contending that the work was too hard, or the boss was impossible, or the hours too long. He never considered marrying any of the many girls he went with, but complained that this one was too demanding, that one was too compliant, and the other one was too this or too that. He would never vote during election because he considered his city's registration and voting regulations too onerous and time-consuming.

I allowed this patient to meander along in therapy for over a year, during which time he gave me a constant stream of excuses for his inability to do one thing or another. I admitted that his excuses had some logic behind them, but kept pointing out that—logic or no logic—he was continually harming himself by his do-nothing attitude. Finally, after I had given him enough rope to hang himself ten times over and he had proceeded to use it for exactly that purpose, he did begin to stick with one job and to develop a good relationship with one girl. I commended him on his progress.

"Yes," he said, "I guess you're surprised to see me going on as steadily as this. Well, let me tell you the reason. I've been with you for eighteen months now—which I understand is rather long for your psychotherapy patients. But let me say that there's one thing I've learned in those eighteen months, and if I never learn anything else as a result of this process, that one thing will remain with me for the rest of my life."

"What is that?" I asked.

"Simply that, although I still find getting up and going to work every morning is hardly the most pleasurable thing in the world, I now know, and shall remember for all time to come, that *not* working is much worse than working."

"You mean?"

"I mean that while working steadily and assuming certain responsibilities may sometimes be rather painful—though I must admit that they're getting less painful as I do them more—*not* working and *not* assuming those responsibilities makes me, as I guess you have been trying to get me to see all along, and as I have resisted seeing until now—well, *not* working is far more painful than working. I absolutely loathe myself when I don't work, and self-loathing is the most painful thing anyone can experience."

Alcoholism and drug addiction. Alcohol and drugs are two of the best pharmacological aids to escapism and to temporary reduction of anxiety. Unfortunately, they both boomerang on their users, since they lead to difficulties which invariably create increased disturbance and hence lead to a need for still larger doses.

Even when drugs and alcohol temporarily work, the user knows that he himself, without their aid, cannot do the things of which he is afraid, and so he obtains no real increase in self-confidence. Indeed, the fact that he has to use these methods of release makes him hate himself all the more, and the usual vicious neurotic circle results.

A typical alcoholic whom I treated had an excellent position in which he was supervised by a domineering, rigid overseer. He liked the work but hated the overseer. He was loath to face this hatred openly, however, because it too closely resembled his feelings toward his own father, who had been a person somewhat similar to his present supervisor. To avoid this conflict, my patient frequently would not show up for work, giving himself the excuse that he did not feel well.

His absences became so frequent that he grew ashamed of phoning in the morning and saying that he was ill, whereupon his supervisor would call him to find out why he had not shown up. He became so afraid to face these calls that he would drink himself into insensibility so that he could not hear the phone ring, or would sit immovably staring at it while he counted the number of rings. Then, when the phone finally stopped ringing or when he woke from his drunken stupor, he would be so ashamed of not having gone to work in the first place, and not being able to talk to his supervisor in the second place, that he would go on a binge for several days. After he sobered up, he would go back to work for a while; but then the same pattern of absenteeism and drinking would began again—a pattern that inevitably led to still more escapism and still more drinking. Only when he was able to face his unconscious hostility toward his father and to realize he had transferred these resentments to his boss, was he able to begin to understand himself. Then, with the aid of rational psychotherapy, he was enabled to attack his own childish beliefs—especially the belief that he *should* have a loving, kind father-boss. And when at last he was able to stop blaming himself and others, he lost his compulsive need to drink.

Self-abasement and self-punishment. As if all their other neurotic traits were not bad enough, some disturbed persons literally try to punish themselves for their assumed sins—including the sin of being neurotic. Starting with unrealistic, perfectionist assumptions that make them feel that they are wicked or inferior, these neurotics live up to their own false picture of themselves by doing things they think they should not do or not doing things they think they should. Then, noting their own weakness or "badness," they punish themselves further by doing something weaker or meaner. This leads them to have still less self-confidence, thereby keeping the ball rolling steadily downhill.

As a grim example of a self-punitive individual, I keep remembering an administrative assistant at an institution where I worked. He felt that marital sex relations were permissible only when they resulted in childbearing. Being, however, always on the brink of financial insolvency, he and his wife could not afford to add to their brood of four children, and therefore they regularly employed birth-control procedures. The husband felt so guilty about this that he would frequently quarrel with his wife during the day, thus making it impossible for them to have satisfactory sex relations at night. On the few occasions when he did succeed in having marital intercourse, he somehow managed either to be ineffectual or not to enjoy himself when he was effective.

One of my patients who was frantically trying to lose weight kept backsliding on her diet. Often, after having eaten a little more than her diet allowed, she would deliberately punish herself by going on to eat half a box of candy or drink several bottles of beer. Only when she was able to take a more realistic attitude toward human failings and to accept herself nonpunitively was she able to make any headway with dieting.

What we have been saying in this chapter about troubled people essentially boils down to this: A neurotic is an individual who theoretically has the capacity to be effective, creative, and free from sustained or exaggerated anxiety and hostility. However, because he has one or more significant irrational, unrealistic assumptions—such as the philosophy that he *must* be universally approved, or that he *should not* be frustrated, or that *it is terrible* if he fails at something he would like to do—the neurotic creates in himself, and then keeps sustaining by constant negative self-talk, various unpleasant and self-harming emotions.

When the neurotic creates and sustains uncomfortable feelings like overconcern, inappropriate anger, groundless guilt, overtenseness, needless feelings of inadequacy, and prolonged depression, he has his choice of consciously experiencing these self-sabotaging emotions and/or setting up unconscious defenses against them. His defenses may include self-deceit, projection, rationalization, evasiveness, psychosomatic complaints, alcoholism, drug addiction, antisocial behavior, compensation, or other forms of escapism.

In most instances, because he has a general philosophy of blame and atonement, the neurotic first hates himself for not being the perfect creature he thinks he should be; and then, once he has developed unhappy feelings or ineffectual behavior, he *also* hates himself for being disturbed. A vicious circle is thereby perpetuated: as a result of unrealistic beliefs the neurotic behaves badly, blames himself still further for thus behaving, and consequently becomes even more neurotic.

3

HOW EMOTIONAL
DISTURBANCES ORIGINATE

In order to be able to live successfully with an emotionally disturbed individual, you should know some details about why and how he became disturbed. Let us now look into this why and how.

No one, as far as we know, is born neurotic, although there may be some inherited factors which make it easier for one person to grow up to be disturbed, while another person, living under even more harrowing circumstances, develops into a relatively untroubled adult. In the main, however, neurosis is bred rather than born; it is learned in the course of one's early life.

We learn to become neurotic as a result of our upbringing. Neurosis, like syphilis and the measles, is a social ailment. We catch it from our parents and from those around us. We are raised by other human beings, and they literally teach us to become neurotic.

Our first propulsions toward neurosis arise out of the attitudes toward ourselves and others that we learn in childhood. Neurotics, essentially, are those who have irrational attitudes, who believe that certain conditions (such as being loved or doing well) which *may* exist, *should* or *must* exist, and that certain other conditions (such as being frustrated or being forced to shift for oneself) which *may not* exist, *should not* or *must not* exist. As a result of their unrealistic ideas, they invariably wind up by hating themselves and others.

All ideas about oneself and others, however, are acquired or learned; and originally they are learned from one's parents or other people who wield influence in a child's early life. Most of what we call an individual's *self* is not just *him*self: it is part of his interaction with other human beings, his *social* self. A person learns that he has certain qualities which distinguish him from others, and he learns this *from* these others. Thus, he learns that one type of person is "handsome" and another "ugly"; that one kind of man is "bright" and another "stupid"; and so on. And he learns that on various scales of handsomeness-ugliness or brightness-stupidity, he himself tends to stand at a certain point, while others stand at different points.

This learning, incidentally, is somewhat relative or accidental, since what a person learns may be quite different if he happens to be raised in one part of the world, or in one family, rather than in another. In one community, for example, he may learn that men with dark skins are "handsome" and that he, having a very dark skin, is quite "handsome"; on the other hand, if he happens to be raised in another community, he may learn that men with dark skins are "ugly" and that he, having a very dark skin, is very "ugly."

Therefore, a man's attitude toward himself, or self-concept, tends to be dependent on the concepts prevalent in the particular community, region, and family in which he is raised. And if he is raised to believe that intelligence and beauty are worth-while traits, and that he is a bright and handsome child, he will tend to look upon himself as "good" and to have a favorable self-concept. But if he is raised to believe that he is stupid and ugly, he will tend to look upon himself as "bad" and to have a poor self-concept. Whether he actually is intelligent or good-looking may have relatively little to do with how he judges himself in these respects, for he may be so favorably or unfavorably biased by the attitudes of others that he unthinkingly accepts their views of him, even though these views happen to be incorrect.

One's early self-concepts, in other words, depend

largely on the concepts that others have toward him—
on the propaganda that they surround him with. If
those who are important in the life of a child generally
blame him, he will learn to blame himself; if they consistently accept him, he will tend to accept himself.
This does not mean that the self-concept a child first
learns is absolutely final and crucial; he can, later in
life, change it for better or worse. But this early self-
concept is most important, and it does tend to set
the pattern for later attitudes and behavior.

Because in our society we have considerably more
don't's than *do's* for children, and because we are consistently telling them that they are wicked or naughty
when they dirty our rugs, kick over our vases, refuse to
go to sleep on time, and so on, we tend to raise millions
of our youngsters—in fact, virtually all of them—with
fairly negative concepts of themselves. It is these negative concepts, or the resulting feelings of inadequacy,
which form one of the central cores of later neuroses.

Putting it differently, we might say that the main
way in which we tend to control children's behavior
today is not by beating or punishing them, but by
explaining to them that certain of their acts are
"wrong" or "bad" and that no one, especially their
parents, will love or approve of them if they continue
to engage in these acts. In raising children in this manner, we wittingly or unwittingly teach them—or propa-
gandize them—to accept several important proposi-

tions: (a) that they should be "good"; (b) that it is disastrous if they are not "good"; (c) that they should try to win the love and approval of virtually everyone; and (d) that it is tragic if they fail to win the love and approval of even a single human being.

If children are well indoctrinated with these premises and permitted to grow up without their being modified, they are virtually doomed to neurosis. They will then almost certainly spend the rest of their days trying to do the impossible: always be "good" and always win the love and approval of everyone. And, since inevitably they will not succeed at these impossible tasks, they will acquire deep-seated feelings of inadequacy and self-hatred, on the one hand, and of frustration and hostility on the other.

Most of the people who come to see me about their difficulties of everyday living are distinctly above the average in intelligence and ability, since in our society psychotherapeutic help is still largely sought by individuals with higher educational backgrounds. Yet almost all my able and talented patients are utterly convinced that they are seriously deficient in several significant respects.

Perhaps the most tragic case of this nature was that of a college student who was unusually tall and handsome, who was in the so-called genius class as far as his tested Intelligence Quotient was concerned, and who composed music and painted so well that all his teachers

were convinced he would become an outstanding crafts-
man in both these fields. Yet this boy not only considered himself so unworthy of female companionship
that he never tried to date any girls, but he also carried
on homosexual activities with the most stupid and least
cultured young ruffians he could find, for fear that he
would not be accepted by better companions.

In this boy's background, which is not atypical,
was a social-register mother who turned over his upbringing almost entirely to nursemaids and servants
and who never stopped criticizing them and her son
whenever the boy did anything that was not strictly
"proper" or "manly." On one particular occasion,
when the boy was given too much to drink by some
guests at one of her parties and then fell asleep on a
bench in the patio and wet his pants while sleeping,
she unceremoniously awoke him and roundly shamed
him in front of the guests. On another occasion, she
found him playing in her clothes closet, and viciously
accused him of spying on her undressing, a circum-
stance which did not happen to be true.

To make matters worse, this boy's father, rarely at
home, was having obvious affairs with other women.
He finally divorced his wife when the son was nine
years old, and showed absolutely no interest in seeing
the boy again, even ignoring invitations to the son's
grade school and prep school graduations. The main
picture that the son had of himself, therefore, was that

which he had viewed through his parents' eyes: a weak, troublesome child who was always a bother to have around and who merited no particular love or attention.

All the young man's later-developed talents and abilities could not overcome his early-acquired concept of himself. He objectively acknowledged that he was good at this thing or that, including his composing and painting, but he could not see himself as a worth-while, essentially lovable person. He was always surprised that I, as his therapist, accepted him for himself, apart from his accomplishments; and it was partly through this kind of acceptance that he finally began to change his self-concepts and to develop emotional relationships with individuals, including females, of his own intellectual and social class.

If an individual reaches maturity with severe feelings of self-blame, he is in a sad plight and there are only a few constructive things he can do. He can, for example, examine the origins of his negative self-concepts, and learn to realize that he was unfortunately taught these by the people close to him in his early life, and that his teachers may not have been correct in their judgments. Then he can set about de-propagandizing himself by consistently showing himself that he really is not "bad," and that he can act "better." He may, especially in active practice, come to accept his early "badness" while consistently working to correct his behavior so that it turns into "goodness." He may also seriously question whether, assuming that he often does "bad" things, he is really so unworthy a person, since all human beings are fallible. And finally, though he learns to admit that he does certain "bad" things, he can ask himself whether it is *always* necessary for him to obtain other people's approval by doing "good" ones. In other words, he can learn to question whether it is absolutely necessary to his happiness that he always be loved and approved by others.

These are all possible and constructive approaches to dealing with the problem of believing that one is wicked, or worthless, or unworthy of social approval. Unfortunately, however, few human beings take these positive approaches. The human animal is so constructed that, once he is taught that it is important that he be "good" and win the approval of virtually all his fellows, he goes on accepting the concept quite unthinkingly, builds almost all his behavior around it, and becomes so panicked when he feels in danger of being "bad" or being disapproved of that he is unable to do anything constructive. Instead, he usually takes the destructive or neurotic path and tries desperately to keep winning the approval of others, even at the expense of his own self-esteem.

One of my patients was the only son of two quite disturbed parents who were firm adherents of a political group. Basically, the son cared nothing for the tenets of this group, but he cared very much for the approval of his parents, who insisted that he be an active member of the group. Whenever he became politically inactive or thought of changing to another group, he grew terribly anxious about losing the love of his parents, and as a result, he invariably returned to the fold—and loathed himself for giving up his independent beliefs.

When confronted by his friends with the fact that he did not really believe in his parents' ideals, he would insist that he did believe in them, and would cite his past services to their group. But, somehow, when it came to attending political rallies, he usually became ill just before the meeting, or fell asleep in the midst of it, or otherwise managed not to participate actively. Still, every time he attempted to quit the group, doubts about whether he was doing the right thing overwhelmed him and, until his psychotherapeutic sessions were well under way, he remained in the fold. When he finally decided, as a result of psychotherapy, that it was more important to him to have his own self-respect than the complete approval of his parents, his neurotic behavior ceased and his anxiety disappeared.

Many—perhaps most—people of our time refuse to face the neurotic issue squarely. They erroneously believe that by winning the approval of others, they can overcome the severe feelings of inadequacy with which they grew up themselves. This is a foolhardy notion for several reasons. First of all, feelings of inadequacy are directly related to a person's dire need for approval, and so the more one thinks he needs to be loved or liked by others, the greater feelings of worthlessness he tends to have. At bottom, people lack confidence in themselves precisely because they *think* it is most important that others approve of them, and they are afraid that this approval will not be forthcoming. Consequently, the more one concentrates on winning approval, the more he emphasizes his own inferiority.

Secondly, attempting to bolster one's self-esteem by winning the love of others is, at best, a hazardous means toward a questionable end. If nine people accept a person fully, and he begins to feel confident because of their acceptance, he still can never be sure of how the tenth person will react. And also, even though he wins the love of a father, wife, child, or friend, he can never be sure how long he will retain it. Self-esteem, therefore, that depends largely on what *others* think, rather than on one's own self-acceptance, is an esteem built on shifting sands.

A young matron, after seeing me for a few psychotherapy sessions, came one day pleading pathetically: "Please, Dr. Ellis, tell me what to do. I keep meeting new people all the time, and whenever I meet one I immediately try to impress this person with how good I am. Naturally, after I act like this for a few minutes, and practically stand on my head to show people how bright and charming I am, they probably say to themselves, 'Boy, what an idiot she is! Who does she think she's fooling?' And then I notice their reaction and I make an even greater effort to impress them. I always wind up by making a complete fool of myself. I know exactly what I'm doing while I'm doing it, but I just can't stop myself. What can I do?"

"Do you realize," I asked, "what you're asking me?"

"No. What?"

"What you're really asking me," I said, "is to arrange things somehow so that everyone you meet immediately loves you."

"Yes, I guess that's right; that's what I really want."

"But what you're asking me to do for you is, of course, perfectly ridiculous—for at least two important reasons. In the first place, I can't very well induce anyone—let alone everyone—to love and approve of you."

"No, I guess you can't."

"And there's an even more important reason why I can't help you in this regard. Just suppose I *could* help you gain the love of everyone you met. Suppose I had a magic wand, and just by waving this wand I could arrange things so that as soon as you met a new person, this individual would immediately love you and feel that you were a fine person. Why, I would be doing you the greatest disservice that one human being can do for another! I'd be helping you remain disturbed for the rest of your life."

"What do you mean?"

"Exactly what I said. The very core of your emotional disturbance, like the core of virtually anyone's neurosis, is that you have this dire *need* for being loved, that you think that you simply *must* be loved, and loved by every single person you meet. This *is* your emotional sickness, and as long as you continue to feel this way, you will remain as upset as you are now. If I catered to this sickness of yours—if I gave you what you mistakenly think that you must have—you would continue to be disturbed indefinitely."

"You mean that if I am to become emotionally healthy, I have to rid myself of the need to be approved by everyone I meet? Without getting rid of this need I cannot possibly get better?"

"Exactly. The aim of psychotherapy is not, as so many people assume, to help the patient win the love and approval of everyone he meets. It is, instead, to enable him to get along well in this world *whether or not* other people quickly adore him. Once a person accepts the fact that life can be satisfying even in relatively hostile surroundings, then *nothing* can ever bother him or her too much again (aside, of course, from physical pain and injury). Such a person is then capable of being happy. But as long as anyone believes that happiness depends almost exclusively on what *other* people think, that person is doomed to inevitable disappointment and sorrow. This is what neurosis largely consists of: the erroneous belief that the world will come to an end unless everyone in it loves you at first sight."

"I see," said my patient. And, eventually, she really did see, and made a remarkable improvement in her behavior and her feeling of contentment.

Most people, however, do not see that winning the love of others is infinitely less important than winning their own self-respect. They go through their entire lives missing one of the most significant lessons a human being can learn—namely, that the one surest path to self-approval is not that of gaining the approval of others, but simply of mastering, by one's own hard effort and self-discipline, some difficult tasks or problems, such as becoming vitally absorbed in some persons or things outside oneself, and working energetically to help those persons or to accomplish those things, not because one wants to be loved and approved of for doing so but simply because of the satisfaction of a job well done. Man, at bottom, is a creative animal. Unless he pushes himself ahead to work creatively at something—whether that something be art, science, agriculture, raising a family, playing a good ball game, or what you will—he will not be happy. Happiness is largely a by-product of creative activity, of intense absorption in some person or thing.

Neurotics, alas, almost invariably find themselves in a vicious circle as far as creativity is concerned. Feeling that they are inferior, and desperately needing the approval of others, they are afraid to take chances, afraid to try creative activity because they feel they may fail at it and thereby reap disapproval. Being afraid to try, they have no chance to practice doing things, and having no practice, naturally they lack skill in these things. Then they are doubly or quadruply convinced that they are worthless and inadequate and that they cannot do anything well. This leads to further inaction, further failure, and further self-depreciation.

The same negative feedback results from the neurotic's usual lack of confidence in himself. Feeling that he is impotent at certain things, the disturbed individual has little self-confidence or a low level of aspiration. But there is a direct relationship between one's level of self-confidence or aspiration and one's performance. If a person believes, for example, that he can easily broad-jump nine feet, he can usually approach or achieve this mark. But if he erroneously believes that he can broad-jump only eight feet, he normally will achieve only an eight-foot jump at best.

Neurotics, believing that they will do poorly in this or that task, almost invariably do just about as poorly as they believe they will. Then they turn right around and say: "See? That proves that I can't do it." Actually, it proves nothing of the sort, but merely shows that they have no confidence in themselves and that achievement often depends on self-confidence.

[82]

Anxiety, moreover, usually sabotages efficiency. One who is terribly anxious about speaking well, or reading quickly, or playing the piano effectively will invariably devote only a small part of his energy and concentration to the subject he is trying to master. Instead, he will spend time asking himself: "How am I doing? How is my audience accepting my performance?" And in so concentrating on *how* rather than on *what* he is doing, he will naturally do more poorly in many instances than his capabilities warrant. Here, again, the neurotic takes this poor performance as proof that he *cannot* do well, when the fact is that he *will* not do well because he is overanxious about his performance.

By the same token, people who feel that others are against them (usually because they feel that they are so inherently inferior that others *should* be against them) often act in an unfriendly, hostile manner to these others. Then, of course, other people will quite understandably turn against them, and this is taken as further "proof" of the original hypothesis.

Neurotics get themselves into still another kind of vicious circle by feeling inadequate, erecting some defense—such as withdrawing, rebelling, or rationalizing—against their feeling of inadequacy, and then hating themselves for using this defense. Although a few neurotic defenses, such as compensation, lead to socially approved behavior, most defenses lead to socially disapproved behavior. And the individual who felt so thoroughly inadequate in the first place that he was driven to use such defenses now feels even more ineffectual *because* he uses them. Thus, a great many of my psychotherapy patients severely condemn themselves for being neurotic—when their neurosis itself resulted from their habitual attitude of self-condemnation.

A common tragedy exists on what may be called the secondary level of neurosis, and often becomes an even greater tragedy than the primary neurosis. Consider an example. Norbert felt that he was weak and ugly; that boys did not like him because of his physical weakness, and that girls felt repulsed by his homeliness. Actually, he was neither too puny nor too ungainly, but he *thought* that he was, and that was the important thing.

Because of his erroneous estimate of himself, Norbert avoided games and exercises, especially those that might have revealed to others his undeveloped body and lack of prowess. He also neglected his appearance, feeling that nothing could be done about it to make him better looking. He made it obvious that he did not care about good looks. He was not in that game, either.

As a result of avoiding physical exercise and neglecting his appearance, Norbert actually did become poor at games and he often did look somewhat repulsive. Some of the fellows, consequently, made a few comments about his lack of physical prowess and his appearance, and these comments eventually got back to him—making him more certain that he was a hopeless, ugly weakling.

To defend himself against what he thought were— and what eventually came actually to be—the unkind observations of others, Norbert began to avoid polite society and to hang around with a group of disturbed, not-too-intelligent boys who did considerable drinking and gambling and kept having minor run-ins with the police. Defensively, he soon began to think this behavior "great stuff." But he also realized, half consciously and half unconsciously, that drinking and gambling were socially disapproved and that he would not gain general acceptance by these means. On the contrary, as far as most people were concerned, he was only making things harder for himself—actually, causing people to like him even less.

In the final analysis, then, Norbert began to worry more about his neurotic behavior—his drinking and gambling—than he originally had about his weakness and his poor looks. Ultimately he felt more inadequate than ever, and was, by these increased feelings of inadequacy, driven into even more neurotic behavior. When he finally came to my attention, he had become involved with a dope-peddling ring, and only by virtue of strong psychological and psychiatric recommendation was he saved from serving a term in prison.

Soon after I saw Norbert at the New Jersey State Diagnostic Center, I was consulted in New York about

Jane, who had just been discharged from a girls' reformatory where she had been confined for sexual promiscuity leading to an illegitimate pregnancy and a self-induced abortion. At the time I saw her, Jane was only sixteen.

Jane originally became disturbed because her parents, themselves serious neurotics, neglected her badly and went off for long vacations together while leaving her in the charge of an unsympathetic relative. After several years of this sort of treatment, she became a whiny, destructive child. Among other things, she did quite badly in her schoolwork, although she had always shown superior intelligence in diagnostic tests.

At the reformatory, Jane continued to do poorly in school and therefore she was trained to do menial work, which she loathed. She knew that she wanted some higher-level activity—her main ambition, in fact, was to be a TV script-writer—but because of her school failures, she thought she was totally stupid and incapable of doing anything except the very work she hated. The result was that she felt more and more inadequate and became consistently more disturbed.

Here, in other words, was a girl who originally failed academically because of her severe emotional problems. Then she took her academic failure as proof of her own stupidity. Then she became still more disturbed as a result of seeing this apparent proof. When I first talked to Jane, I found that the original cause of her neurosis —her sensitivity to her father's and mother's rejection—no longer particularly bothered her, since by this time she had become relatively inured to their rejection and even had some insight into how neurotic they were and how they were not to be blamed for neglecting her. But her *secondary* neurosis—her increased feelings of inadequacy caused by the original neurotic symptoms which first made her do badly in school—remained with her and continued to plague her until she had received a considerable amount of psychotherapeutic help.

So it often happens: the individual actually surmounts the first cause of his neurotic symptoms and learns to accept the original circumstances, such as parental rejection, which led to the development of his neurosis. But by this time—by the time he learns to live with his original feelings of inadequacy—these have led him to other socially disapproved behavior, to other mistakes, for which he cannot forgive himself, and which help to make him feel woefully inadequate and to build new neurotic defenses.

Another example: One of my patients hated himself so much and had so little self-confidence, because of his reactions to the continual nagging of his mother, that he tended to stutter fearfully during the day and to lie awake at night worrying about his day's behavior. After a while, even though his mother accepted him and stopped her nagging, he continued to worry about the stuttering and the insomnia.

This patient finally became so concerned about his

neurotic symptoms that his sense of inadequacy increased, and he became a worse stutterer and insomniac, and developed still other neurotic traits. His primary neurosis thus became a focal point for the starting of a secondary neurosis; and his secondary disturbance made him more miserable than the primary one ever had. Up until the time he came for therapy, his neurotic circle not only became vicious but continued to get wider and wider, enveloping more and more of his personality in its terrible sweep.

Does neurosis, as we seem to be implying, arise solely from feelings of inadequacy and self-hatred? Not exactly. It may result from one or more major irrational ideas, several of which lead not only to feelings of worthlessness or lack of self-confidence, but also to exaggerated feelings of hostility, rebelliousness, and tension—which, too, must be included under the heading of neurosis.

What are some of the major irrational assumptions or philosophies which lead human beings into neurotic behavior? In studies of patients (some have been published in professional journals; see the bibliography at the end of this book), I have found that these main irrational ideas include the following:

• An adult must be approved of or loved by almost everyone for almost everything he does; what others think of him is most important; depending on others is better than depending on oneself.

• A person should be thoroughly competent, adequate, talented, and intelligent in all possible respects; the main goal and purpose of life is achievement, success; incompetence in anything whatsoever is an indication that a person is inadequate or valueless.

• One should blame oneself severely for all mistakes and wrongdoings; punishing oneself for errors will help prevent future mistakes.

• A person should blame others for their mistaken or bad behavior; he should get upset by the errors and stupidities of others; one should spend considerable time and energy trying to reform others; one can best help others by roundly criticizing them and sharply pointing out the error of their ways.

• Because a certain thing once strongly affected one's life, it should indefinitely affect it; because a person was once weak and helpless, he must always remain so; because parents or society taught the acceptance of certain traditions, one must go on unthinkingly accepting these traditions.

• If things are not the way one would like them to be, it is a catastrophe; things *should* be better than they are; other people should make things easier for us, help with life's difficulties; no one should have to put off present pleasures for future gains.

• Avoiding life's difficulties and self-responsibilities is easier than facing them; inertia and inaction are necessary and/or pleasant; one should rebel against doing things, however necessary, if doing them is unpleasant.

• Much unhappiness is externally caused or created by outside persons and events; a person has virtually no control over his emotions and cannot help feeling bad on many occasions.

• If something is or may be dangerous or injurious, one should be seriously concerned about it; worrying about a possible danger will help ward it off or decrease its effect.

These major illogical notions may be more briefly summarized by saying that when a person believes that the things he *prefers* or *would like* to have happen *should* or *must* occur, and that it is catastrophic (instead of moderately irritating or "too darned bad") when they do not occur, he is being thoroughly irrational. Why? Because reality is what it is, not what we should like it to be; because the only sane thing to do about an unpleasant situation is either to try to change it or, if it is unchangeable, to accept it. Getting thoroughly upset about an annoying condition—which is essentially the same thing as telling oneself it is a real disaster—will not only fail to improve the condition but usually will help make it considerably worse.

It is important to note that the unrealistic, irrational ideas which cause neurosis are generally, at least in part, unconscious rather than conscious. The individual often consciously knows that it is silly to expect everyone to love him, to hope to do everything perfectly all the time, to be unable to stand any frustration, or to worry about threatening possibilities. But, unconsciously, he firmly and deeply believes this nonsense; and, again unconsciously, he keeps telling himself over and over that he *should* be loved, *must* do well, *should not* be frustrated, *should* worry over possible accidents, and the like. His conscious views, therefore, are seriously in conflict with his unconscious values and philosophies; and, particularly since the latter are unattainable, he will inevitably become upset and begin to act neurotically.

What, it may be asked, about deep-lying complexes such as the Oedipus complex? How do they fit into the neurotic picture?

These unconscious complexes are causative factors in neurosis, *not* in their own right but because they invariably represent (or are the *result* of) serious conflicts in values and ideas. Take the Oedipus complex, for example. According to Freud and his followers, this complex arises because a young boy lusts after his mother, wants to have sex relations with her, is afraid that his father will punish him for his desires, and therefore becomes afraid of and hostile to his father (and other authority figures) and guilty in relation to his mother (and other maternal images).

Suppose that we examine a particular individual and discover that he actually has an Oedipus complex and that he is behaving neurotically because of it. The question still remains: *Why* does he have such a complex? Was he (as Freud thought) virtually doomed to acquire it at birth? Or did he (as most modern psychoanalysts appear to believe) acquire it through his cultural training?

The answer almost certainly is the latter. For the Oedipus complex is merely a description of an individual's neurotic pattern; it is not its basic cause. If, for instance, a young boy lusted after his mother and believed that his feelings were *natural* and *good* instead of *unnatural* and *bad,* how would this attitude affect the situation? Suppose he believed that, if they discovered about his sex desires, his mother and father would be accepting and uncritical instead of horrified and punitive? Under such circumstances, would this boy develop any upsetting complex? Of course not!

The real causes of an Oedipus complex, therefore, are not the mere *facts* that a boy lusts after his mother and that he is in danger of being punished for his feelings; rather, they are his *beliefs,* his *attitudes,* about these facts. And these beliefs are hardly inborn; they result largely from the culture in which he lives. If a child is raised (as, in point of fact, millions of people throughout the world are) with the ideas that it is not very wicked to have incestuous feelings, that his father and mother will not be seriously offended if he does have them, and that he will *not* be punished for

Oedipal attachments, there is little chance that he will become seriously disturbed or develop a debilitating complex, if and when he lusts after his mother.

The basic causes of neurosis, then, are not the unfortunate happenings, dangers, or frustrations that often beset our lives; they are, rather, our own illogical, unrealistic ideas or views about the way things are and the way they supposedly should or must be. Once a person has perfectionist ideologies, one or two major results (as noted in the previous chapter) will inevitably occur: either he will be unnecessarily unhappy (for example, tense, depressed, guilty, or anxious); and/or he will set up defenses against consciously experiencing emotional pain (for example, will rationalize, project, lie, take to alcohol or drugs, or compensate). In other words: the main symptoms of neurosis are needless unhappiness, or behavior that is defensively inhibited, compulsive, or over-impulsive; and its main causes are irrational ideas.

When an individual experiences exceptional tension, despair, anxiety, or other negative feelings, or when he has unusually rigid defenses and has to resort to hallucinations, paranoid thinking, extreme inertia, or other unusual escapes from reality, he is psychotic rather than neurotic. Psychotics are extremely disturbed persons who almost always need intensive professional treatment.

But the great majority of troubled individuals is in

the neurotic rather than the psychotic range. And, if these neurotics are understood and reacted to favorably, they can be helped considerably in most instances, as we shall later show in detail.

4

SOME BASIC FACTORS IN EMOTIONAL UPSETS

In our culture, are human beings practically predestined to acquire deep-seated feelings of inadequacy or low frustration-tolerance early in their lives so that they are predisposed toward neurosis? Theoretically, no. It presumably is possible to raise a child so that he really likes himself, is not obsessed with winning others' approval, and accepts life's difficulties without whining or retreat.

In practice, however, there are many forces in our society that encourage the development of severe inadequacy feelings and emotional upset. Among them are the following:

Parental models. If a child's parents are themselves

inadequate, whining, spineless individuals, he normally will tend to identify himself with them and imitate them in important ways. Thus, he will become something of a woeful replica of them. Or, if he is ashamed of his inadequate parents, he may feel that he comes from inferior stock and is himself therefore "bad."

Mothers (and sometimes fathers) frequently come to me and ask: "What can I do, Dr. Ellis, to help my child? I would do anything if you would only tell me exactly what."

To the mother of a fourteen-year-old girl who asked me this question, I replied: "You say you really want to help your daughter stop being afraid of people and teach her how to make friends. Fine. But did you ever stop to think what kind of people you and your husband yourselves are in this regard? From what you've told me, you are afraid to join your local church group because you think you don't quite measure up to the other women in the group. And your husband, you say, even though he hates it, has stayed at the same job for years, largely because he is terrified at the thought of being interviewed for a new one. No wonder your daughter is afraid of people! When her own parents show her, by deed as well as attitude, that they think contact with others is frightening, how could she help being timid about making friends herself?"

"You think we should do something about ourselves, then?"

"I most certainly do. The best thing you can do to help your daughter is to help yourselves. If you cultivate your *own* garden more adequately, she will see by your good example that it isn't so difficult to cultivate hers. But as long as *you* set her a poor example, how can you expect her to do better?"

Parental models can be exceptionally important in the life of a child. Parents who are themselves ineffectual and inadequate individuals can quite unconsciously cause their children to acquire severe self-deprecatory feelings. And those who catastrophize frustrations will tend to raise spoiled brats who, well on into adulthood, will behave similarly.

Early rejection. One of the easiest ways to give a child serious feelings of inferiority is to reject him: to show that you do not love him and will not help him in important ways. For if a child is highly undervalued by the members of his own family, who presumably—above all others—should accept him, how can he reasonably be expected to value himself properly?

I knew a couple who had a handsome, graceful child whom every relative and friend of the family liked on sight, made a great fuss over, and significantly favored. The couple also had a younger child who was not particularly good-looking or graceful and who therefore received relatively little attention.

The younger child was actually much brighter, in

terms of intelligence tests and the ability to do school-work, than was the older. But the older child, because of the greater self-confidence gained through early approval, believed in himself, thought himself to be exceptionally intelligent, and from an early age began working for a professional degree. Meanwhile, the younger one had little self-confidence, considered his brother brighter than he, and quit school at an early age to become a garage mechanic.

Early rejection by others tends to encourage self-rejection; this, in turn, leads to neurosis. The child tends to like himself just about as much as he thinks others like him.

Criticism. By children, criticism is almost always taken as disapproval. Parents who continually nag a child are indirectly saying: "You are just no good; in fact, you are pretty hopeless." Even though they criticize for the child's "own good," even though they feel that criticism is necessary for teaching purposes, even though their criticism is to some degree justified—no matter: to the child it indicates a lack of approval, a lack of faith in him. Whereupon he most usually begins to show the same lack of faith in himself.

The mother of one of my young female patients would say to her daughter: "Oh, you're not doing the dishes right." Or "Here, let me boil that egg. You'll only ruin it." Or "You go do your homework; I'll iron that dress for you." The mother thought she was helping her daughter, making things easier for her. Actually, she was hindering her enormously, for the daughter always concluded that she could not, of herself, do anything correctly, that she was just no good.

Perfectionism. Teaching a child to be a perfectionist is one of the subtlest and most drastic modes of criticism. For none of us is or can be perfect; and excessive striving to be perfect will inevitably lead to disillusionment, heartache, and self-hatred. Perfectionists must be "good" or "best" in all things at all times—which, of course, is impossible. You might just as well put a rope around a child's neck and tie a wild horse to the other end as to instill in him a too-urgent desire to be perfect or "best."

Speaking of perfectionism recalls to mind another of my patients. She was one of the best-endowed youngsters I have ever seen. At seventeen, when she first visited me, she was so unusually good-looking that any male patients in my waiting room immediately sat up and took notice. This girl had a tested Intelligence Quotient of 178 (a score obtained by about one out of a thousand individuals), and she was a remarkably talented dancer and sculptress. But she thought she was ugly, stupid, and untalented. Why? Because from her earliest school years, whenever she came home with 97 or 98 in some subject, her mother, thoroughly unimpressed, would immediately complain: "So! And why couldn't it be 100?" As a result, the girl had such a low estimate of herself that she was in the borderline psychotic range.

Another patient, whose parents pointedly would associate only with the "best" people, obtained fabulously good grades in all his college subjects—except art. Not only was he unable to draw or paint very well; he even seemed unable to appreciate artistic masterpieces. This bothered him, and he took one art course after another in order to prove to himself that he could succeed at them. And whenever he received, as he invariably did, a mediocre grade, he was genuinely disturbed. He insisted that he should do well in *everything*, and that something must be wrong with him if he did not. I had a hard time getting him to adopt a more realistic attitude toward himself.

Competitiveness. In our culture, perfectionism often takes the form of extreme competitiveness. We teach a child that he should be *better* than other children and should grow up to be a *bigger* success. Statistically, of course, this is impossible since only a few outstanding individuals can actually be consistently better than their fellows. The inevitable result is that millions of Americans try frantically to keep up with the Joneses, or the champions, or the millionaires; and most of them end up feeling disappointed and inadequate.

"Why," I ask my friends, relatives, and patients, "why must you be *better* than this one or that one?"

"Well, I just feel uncomfortable if I'm not."

"But why do you feel uncomfortable? What good does it really do you to be better than someone else?"

"I don't know. I just feel that way."

"But *why* do you feel that way?"

"I really can't say. I guess I haven't ever thought about the reason."

"Exactly! You have merely *accepted* the notion without thinking about it. The real reason, of course, is that you have been taught to believe that being better or greater than someone else is a very good thing. And, unhesitatingly believing this propaganda, you automatically act upon it and are woefully unhappy when you are not better or greater than someone else. That's the tragedy: you are unhappy because you don't think about what you are taught."

This I say to my friends, relatives, and patients. Sometimes it does some good.

Unnecessary taboos. One of the main reasons people are insecure is because they feel guilty—because they think they have done something wrong or wicked. Thus, the more things they have been taught are wrong, the more taboos they have, the guiltier and more overwhelmed with feelings of inadequacy they are going to be. Our particular society carries on innumerable sexual, social, racial, religious, and other taboos which once had a rationale, but which today are clearly outmoded. As a result, hordes of our citizens feel inordinately guilty and self-hating.

Take, by way of illustration, one of my acquaintances. (I shall call him Mr. Potter.) Mr. Potter was raised by very "good," exceptionally strict parents. From early childhood, they taught him that he should not be rowdy, nor engage in any kind of sex play whatever, nor talk back to his elders, nor have a good time when there was any kind of work to be done, nor do any one of dozens of various things.

The list of don't's in Mr. Potter's early life was thick enough to choke a human being. It did. When I met him, in his thirtieth year, Mr. Potter was doing miserably in his business, was completely impotent with his wife, was a tyrant with his son and daughter, and was troubled in almost every conceivable way. The taboos with which he had been raised had made him feel like a villain when he didn't adhere to them closely, and like a sissy when he did.

On both counts, Mr. Potter felt most inadequate. He was as constricted an individual as I have ever met, having narrowed down his positive enjoyments to sub-zero proportions, and having replaced them with neurotic symptoms.

Sigmund Freud, one of the greatest psychologists, saw very clearly the terrible effects which unnecessary taboos can have on human beings. Unfortunately, prejudiced by the special sex taboos of the middle-class Viennese of the 1890's, Freud overemphasized the sexual aspects of neurosis, and at times implied that sex guilt was at the bottom of all human inadequacy feelings. This, especially when applied to today's slightly more liberal sex attitudes, is something of an overstatement. Freud was quite right, however, in stressing that *some* kind of taboo is behind most of our guilt feelings; and that these feelings of guilt, in their turn, underlie much of our emotional perplexity.

Spoiling. Overprotecting a child can be just as disastrous to its self-esteem as rejecting it. For children who are spoiled and who have everything done for them may grow up to believe that things *should* be this way, and may never attempt to do anything for themselves. Or they may simply get no practice in taking chances, experimenting, and putting their ideas into action, and consequently they become inept at doing so. When they finally discover that the world is a fairly rough place in which to live, they feel incapable of coping with it and begin to experience deep-seated feelings of inferiority.

Getting along well in life, like virtually all aspects of living, requires learning, practice, and effort. If, by the time one reaches his teens and begins to think independently, he has had little previous experience in making decisions, he naturally finds the going intolerably rough. This is exactly what would happen if, say, a boy tried at the age of sixteen to play baseball when in his entire previous life he had never thrown a ball or any other object.

To make matters even worse, one sees other people who have had plenty of experience and practice do things routinely and automatically. Without any great difficulty, they ease their way over paths that appear, to the inexperienced to be filled with unconquerable hurdles. Then, those who have been coddled and over-protected as children say to themselves: "Why can't *I* do things that well, that easily? What's wrong with *me?*" This situation, of course, leads to even more intense feelings of inferiority.

An extreme example of this condition was the case of a man who, at one and the same time, had been over-protected *and* rejected, spoiled *and* disapproved of by his parents during his childhood. When I saw him, at the age of forty, he was unable after literally thirty-five years of schooling to accept a job as an assistant professor of English literature, although theoretically he was thoroughly qualified.

This man had had the grave misfortune to be thoroughly rejected by his father, who wanted him to be a sportsman instead of a scholar, and who never failed to criticize the boy for not being what he, the father, had always dreamed a son of his should be. To make matters infinitely worse, however, while criticizing the son on the one hand, he continually attempted to bribe the boy with money and presents on the other hand, so that the son always got everything he wanted without ever having to strive for anything.

As a result, the son doubly disliked himself—because his father despised him, and because he knew that he always accepted his father's bribes and never attempted to do anything for himself. And, since he had never really buckled down to doing anything difficult, at the age of forty he was still without the necessary experience that would ultimately make such difficult tasks easy. Hence, he was loath to accept the professorial job for which he was actually well qualified.

Spoiling may lead to two major types of disordered emotions: self-hatred and inability to tolerate frustration. The spoiled individual may lose confidence in himself, or may refuse to accept the necessary frustrations and unchangeable annoyances of everyday living and become extremely irritable and hostile. Either or both ways, the fact that his parents neglected to teach him to accept some of the grim realities of life may do him much harm.

Frustration. Just as giving a child everything he wants may spoil him and encourage his avoidance of life's responsibilities, so giving him nothing and continually frustrating him may also lead to his acquiring a negative, unrealistic attitude. The human is, whether we like it or not, a distinctly limited animal, and even though he can tolerate huge amounts of frustration, he does have a breaking point. This is particularly true of a young child, who cannot stand the kind of frustrations often imposed by overly rigid parents. Under deeply frustrating circumstances, a child can be forced into activities which he loathes, but he may thus lose confidence and develop serious feelings of resentment.

One of my former secretaries, the youngest of thirteen children, had a father who worked steadily but who never made enough money to satisfy the material needs of his large family. The mother did her best for all the children, but this best was none too good, in view of the enormous difficulties involved. The girl, consequently, never had the toys, clothes, spending money, leisure, or other advantages which the other children in her neighborhood had. Very little of what she wanted was she ever able to get.

This girl grew up feeling unloved; she believed that life was supremely unfair to her and her family, and that there was little point in going on in such a life when it offered so little. Instead of trying to work harder (which would have been the logical thing to do in view of the family's economic needs) she soon gave up, viewed the situation as hopeless, and spent by far the greater part of her time bewailing her fate instead of trying to better it.

One of my patients came from a family where he was the only child in a well-to-do home. But his parents, who themselves came up through life the hard way, were stiff-spined New Englanders who did not believe in earthly pleasures. They leaned over backward not to spoil their child—gave him virtually no toys during his entire childhood, provided him with only a niggardly allowance, and looked with enormous disfavor on any plans for amusement he might want to carry out.

This man, too, almost exactly like the girl from the very poor family, soon felt so frustrated that he hardly knew which way to turn. He finally gave up trying, sabotaged his parents' desires for his success in life by refusing to work at anything, and failed miserably, first at school and then at a series of mediocre jobs. He could not see why, in view of the lack of earthly rewards for "good" behavior, he should work his head off for nothing. So he went on the common, garden-variety emotional sit-down strike, refusing to do anything he didn't have to do—and thereby, of course, hurting himself as well as his parents.

Suppressed hostility. A particular kind of frustration which many individuals cannot stand arises when they forcefully hate someone or something but feel constrained to suppress or repress their hostility. Such suppressed hatred generally leads to internal simmering and seething, a transference of aggression to someone or something else, or a final, violent outburst of the suppressed feelings.

A young psychologist whom I was supervising frothed and fumed because the head of the institution where he worked restricted his activities in so many ways. Not being able to do anything about this situation, the young man tended at first to act aggressively toward the inmates of the institution. When this was pointed out to him and he was warned against transferring his aggression in this manner, he went on a wild driving spree one day, punched a policeman who arrested him for speeding, and wound up in the county jail. Fortunately, the judge before whom he appeared had himself had psychotherapy. He placed the psychologist on probation, with the proviso that he receive intensive treatment.

The interesting thing is that when this psychologist did receive therapeutic help—which, in any event, he ultimately intended to obtain as part of his training—he was able to function quite effectively in the same institution and under the same restrictive conditions which had previously been so upsetting. For he then took the new attitude that the administrator himself had his own emotional difficulties, and consequently could only be expected to act in the authoritative fashion in which he had been acting. Accepting this, the young psychologist was able to refrain from getting angry or having to suppress his anger or to replace it with aggressive behavior.

In many important ways, therefore, our society in general and our family-centered manner of raising children in particular tend to encourage us to think unrealistically and illogically and to develop inordinate feelings of inadequacy and resentment. Then, we blame ourselves so severely for being ineffective or hostile that we often erect neurotic defenses against admitting these faults. In turn, our defenses effectively prevent us from tackling the irrational ideas behind our difficulties and doing something constructive about them.

Most neurosis, at bottom, seems to be caused by irrational or exaggerated fear—we generally call it anxiety. Rational fear is that which exists when a person is actually in danger, as in fearing to cross a busy street without looking to see whether a car is coming. Irrational fear, or anxiety, is the fear one has when he is not in great danger or when he exaggerates the likelihood or degree of a possible danger, as a person does when he fears walking on the sidewalk because he thinks a car might mount the curb and hit him.

The two things that are commonly feared by human beings are physical injury or annihilation and social disapproval. In comparison to primitive days, life today offers fewer chances of physical injury, for modern medical science, police forces, and protective devices have minimized such dangers. On the other hand, recent developments in atomic science and its war potential, and death-dealing automobile accidents have led to the growth of new physical fears.

The second prevalent human fear, that of social disapproval, seems to be becoming more important with the years, since in some ways we now have more needs for conformity, for being like others, for keeping up with the Joneses, than our forefathers had. More and more, we are literally raising our children to think that being loved or approved of is the greatest good in the world; and less and less, in many respects, are we raising them to strive for self-approval, self-mastery, and a vital absorption in intrinsically interesting, creative work.

The need for social approval is primarily taught in the family setting. As soon as the child does anything wrong—that is, anything the parents disapprove of or find inconvenient—there is a tendency for his father or mother to pounce on him and say, "Don't do that, dear. If you do that *people won't love you.*" Or "*. . . nobody will like you.*" Or "*. . . Mother won't like it.*" These phrases are usually said in such threatening tones, and are so often backed up with a reproving slap or gesture, that the child quickly gets the idea that it is *terrible, horrible, awful,* if people—and especially his parents—do not like him. And for the rest of his life he tends to retain this early-acquired belief, and never to question it in any way.

We also raise our children to blame themselves in many ways, particularly for their socially disapproved behavior. We give them a literature, from fairy tales to TV shows, that is replete with villains, "bad men," and wicked witches. We teach them to hate, to blame these villains, and to loathe themselves when they are "villainous."

Actually, of course, there are no villains, since individuals who engage in dastardly acts only do so because they either inherited a tendency toward such behavior or were raised to be the way they are. If they are *born* wicked, they certainly shouldn't be blamed. And if they are raised to be culprits, like John Dillinger and Adolf Hitler, they still are not to be blamed for the way they are, but instead should be understood psychologically and helped to get over their emotional disturbances.

Because, however, of an adherence to ancient ideologies formulated long before there was any knowledge of modern dynamic psychology, society still retains the concept of holding human beings personally responsible for their crimes and of demanding that they atone for their sins through being punished. And this punishment is demanded not only of external "villains" but of oneself when he does wrong things.

Such a punitive philosophy makes all of us enormously guilty about many of the things we do, and guilt is but another name for feelings of inadequacy or self-hatred. This is not to say, of course, that no one should ever feel culpable about his behavior. Whenever one needlessly, gratuitously, and willfully harms another human being, he should fully acknowledge the wrongdoing. But, even then, he should feel guilty only in the sense of resolving not to perpetrate such actions again, rather than in the sense of resolving to punish himself.

In other words, there are two essential ways of handling guilt feelings, one rational and legitimate, and the other not. The rational way is by the acceptance of wrongdoing or culpability. Thus, if one needlessly harms another person (as by stealing from or physically hurting him) one should quickly acknowledge his guilt —that is, his responsibility for the act. One should say to himself: "Yes, I committed that offense against John. I was wrong."

The irrational way of dealing with guilt is, after having acknowledged wrongdoing, going on from there and saying to oneself: "I *should not* have done that wicked deed against John. I'm a villain for doing it. It's unforgivable for me to have committed that crime. I must be punished for doing it."

This reaction to guilt is irrational because, first of all, it is silly for a person to tell himself that he *should not* have committed a wicked deed when, quite obviously, he *did*. What one really means is: *"It would have been better* if I had not committed the deed." Doubtless it would have been. But changing the sentence *"It would have been better* if I had not done this,"* into "I *should not* have done it," is akin to locking the barn after the horse has been stolen, and makes no real sense. It implies that there is some immutable, God-given law against being immoral, and this is an hypothesis for which there is no factual evidence, and which can never be proved or disproved.

Secondly, telling oneself: "I'm a villain for acting

badly toward John, and I should be punished for being so villainous," implies that punishment will do some good—that is, will help right the wrong done to John, and will help prevent the wrongdoer from harming John (or someone else) again. Actually, of course, no matter how the guilty one is punished, John is not likely to be benefited. And the whole history of human punishment shows that in reality punishing and blaming human beings for their sins does not very effectively prevent them from doing evil things again.

The reason blame and punishment normally do not change people for the better is that they induce the culprit to bemoan his *past* deeds rather than to concentrate on how to change them *in the future*. If a person tells himself repeatedly, "Oh, what a villain I am for hurting John," how can he possibly focus his attention on the real problem, which is: "How can I avoid hurting John (and others) in the future?" The fact is that he can't.

Finally, even though one is guilty in the sense that he has needlessly harmed John, it is still questionable whether he is guilty in the sense that he easily could have avoided injuring John, and cavalierly chose to hurt him. As we noted before, immoral behavior stems from either inherited tendencies toward criminality (in which few psychologists believe today) or from faulty learning. And if a person inherited or learned a tendency to hurt others, why should he be *blamed* for having that inclination? He is as much a victim of his deed, in many ways, as is John.

What should one do under such circumstances? The best thing to do is to make the rational and legitimate observation: "I harmed John and I was wrong for doing so." Then, instead of irrationally continuing, "I'm a villain and deserve to be punished for this deed," continue with, "Granted that I did wrong this time, how can I make amends to John for my misdeeds, and how, especially, can I prevent myself from harming John again *next time?*"

If this is the tack one takes, if he focuses on how to *change* his poor behavior in the future instead of how to punish himself for past misdeeds, the chances are excellent that he will soon figure out a way to be less immoral. But if one focuses on self-blame and punishment, he will almost inevitably miss the real point— which is *learning* from one's wrongdoings—and continue to perpetrate them indefinitely.

The basis of rational morality, in other words, lies in two main propositions: first, that if one needlessly harms others, the chances are good that these others or their associates will retaliate in kind, and the chaotic, harm-dealing world that will then tend to exist will be a rather frightful place for all of us to live in; second, that if and when one does unnecessarily hurt someone, he should quickly acknowledge his antisocial behavior and immediately set about *changing* it for the better.

Unfortunately, however, most moralists in human history have changed these two propositions into a significantly different form, and have contended that when one human being harms another, he is going against some "natural" or "necessary" law of God and man, and that when anyone flouts this law, he is wicked and should mercilessly be condemned and punished either by himself or others.

Actually, we are not necessarily immoral when we harm someone else—for the good reason that in the society in which we live, it is often *necessary* that we harm another in order to survive ourselves. Thus, if a man takes a seat in a crowded train or makes a profit on selling a house, he may be benefiting at the expense of others. But as long as he does not needlessly, deliberately, go out of his way to *harm* others, he is not immoral. If one man really has acted vilely toward another, beating himself over the head will hardly right the wrong he has done. The only sensible procedure is for him to resolve, in the present and in the future, to help the person he has harmed—or at least to refrain from harming him.

Negative self-blame, then, only results in neurosis-producing feelings of inadequacy. It does nothing to right any evil one has done. On the contrary, it generally prevents one from doing anything about correcting his wrongs—and thereby leads him to further self-blame. Positive, constructive regard for the present and future is the only logical solution to the problem of moral behavior; and such a solution is exactly what our concepts of "villainy" and punishment inevitably sabotage.

In the last analysis, neurosis is usually a moral problem, and Sigmund Freud was essentially correct when he viewed it as a conflict between what he called the superego (or conscience) and man's unconscious strivings (his id) on the one hand, and his conscious desires (his ego) on the other. Freud, however, made too much of man's sexual and biological drives and conflicts, and too little of his nonsexual, socially learned impulses.

But the fact still remains that when human beings feel certain aspects of their behavior are wrong or wicked, and when, instead of doing something constructive about changing these activities, they merely berate themselves for continuing to perform them, they invariably end up by hating themselves—and their self-hatred sends them along the road of defensiveness and symptom-building which we call neurosis. Then, in turn, their very neurotic traits cause them, in most instances, to hate themselves still more, and to become more defensive and more neurotic. Here we have a circle that, in terms of the construction and maintenance of a healthy, productive, happy personality, is not merely vicious; it is positively lethal.

5

HOW TO HELP A TROUBLED PERSON OVERCOME HIS DISTURBANCE

The best way to live with a neurotic is to help him overcome his neurosis. Is this possible? Can an emotionally disturbed individual actually get better? be effectively cured? Categorically, yes. But it is certainly not easy.

It is possible for a neurotic to get over his disturbance, and for another person to help him do so, because the disturbance invariably stems from irrational, unrealistic ideas which are learned rather than inherited, and which (with some difficulty) can be unlearned or changed. Moreover, neurotic symptoms such as exaggerated and sustained feelings of anxiety, anger, tension, guilt, and depression are nothing but reactions to or effects of illogical thinking. A neurotic can be helped to overcome these symptoms by encouraging him to change his thinking.

Although the irrational thinking which leads to neurosis is largely unconscious, it is not, as the orthodox Freudians believe, so deeply hidden and repressed that it cannot be brought to consciousness without a long therapeutic process. Irrational ideas like the idea that one should not be frustrated or must be competent in all ways can often be brought to the surface of a neurotic's consciousness by showing him that his disordered behavior proves that he must have these ideas. The difference between his rational, conscious beliefs and his disturbed behavior is his irrational unconscious beliefs.

Once a neurotic is helped to see that he is being irrational in some of his fundamental beliefs, he can also be helped to attack these beliefs, in many instances, by showing him how silly they are, by inducing him to act against them, and by other techniques which will be described in this chapter. All this, we must frankly admit, may be difficult but it is still quite possible.

It is not easy to change or "cure" neurotics because frequently they do not wish to admit, in the first place, that they are disturbed. And even when they will admit it, they often refuse outside help and insist that they will help themselves. Sometimes when they do want to be helped, they unconsciously resist help because they are so accustomed to their own symptoms that they are blinded to the details of these symptoms. And sometimes they resist help because they are so ashamed of their neurotic behavior that they have difficulty facing it.

Neurotic habits are two-edged: they are motivated by some irrational idea; and they become the embodiment of that idea in some semi-rational practice. To overcome such neurotic habits, one must work on both the underlying idea and the practice. A boy, for example, stutters because he is afraid of what other people think of his speech patterns. But even if he gets over this fear of stuttering, he still has the motor habit of stuttering (perhaps of many years standing) to overcome. Naturally this is difficult.

If a neurotic habit is squelched or suppressed without getting at its underlying cause, it may be replaced by another equally obnoxious habit. Thus, if a boy stutters because he is afraid, let us say, that he will utter nasty words, and he merely works on the habit of stuttering, he may overcome that habit but still have the fear of saying nasty words. In such a case, he may develop some other neurotic symptom, such as attacks of colitis or a fear of going visiting. That is why many psychotherapists are reluctant to use hypnosis, simple reassurance, drugs, and certain other techniques which sometimes cure a neurotic habit or symptom without getting at the root of the individual's neurosis and changing his basic personality pattern.

Neurosis originating in irrational assumptions, consists of disordered emotions and/or defensive behavior which prevent the disturbance of an individual from conscious recognition. To conquer a neurosis, one must understand it fully and attack its ideational origins, and also work through the ensuing habitual symptoms. Occasionally, insight into the causes of one's symptoms quickly and automatically leads to clearing them up. Much more often, however, insight merely lays the groundwork for changing one's ideologies and undoing one's symptoms. Their actual eradication requires much further work—and *work* is the word of choice here—on the part of the neurotic individual.

Relatives and friends may be particularly helpful in aiding neurotics because, unlike a psychotherapist who sees his patients a few hours a week, they see the disturbed individual continuously, and often by their own attitudes toward his disturbance, they can help to reduce it. In my own psychotherapeutic work, I frequently use my patients' associates as auxiliary therapists and sometimes find that I can succeed better through their efforts than directly by means of my own. This is particularly true with young children, who can be treated largely by working with their parents; but it is also true of many so-called adults.

Trying to help neurotics with whom one is closely

associated is difficult because, among other things, it requires several traits and some knowledge not too commonly found existing together in the average person. For example, the helper himself should not be too neurotic; if he is, he will tend to have many problems of his own and will be so emotionally involved and nonobjective that he can be of little aid to anyone else. The helper should have considerable patience and energy to devote to his task of helping the disturbed person. He should have keen insight into human behavior and understand both himself and others to some degree. He should not expect to treat his neurotic friends and relatives as a therapist would treat a patient, because his relationship to the neurotic is usually much more personal and involved than are the relations of a professional therapist and those he treats.

The very first step toward helping an individual become less neurotic is for the prospective helper to recognize clearly and to *accept* the fact that the individual is neurotic. Most people who have close associations with disturbed relatives or friends simply refuse to accept the fact that these people are disturbed, and they continue to treat them as if they were well-adjusted. Disaster inevitably ensues. For neurotics are not well adjusted. And if one treats them as if they were able to live up to the kinds of behavior expected of non-neurotics, they will quickly disappoint him. Then, if one shows his disappointment, the neurotic will feel that he has failed—hence, he will tend to become more neurotic.

Accepting a neurotic's emotional disturbance is not easy. As was explained in the first chapter, disturbed people are often unreliable, hostile, ungrateful, self-centered, and unloving. Trying to accept them the way they are often is like trying to live with a blackguard or an enemy. But, if one is going to help them, this acceptance simply *must* be given, and given almost without reservation.

Of course, one does not *have* to accept a neurotic, even a close relative like a sister or a husband. Except for the children whom one voluntarily brought into the world and in consequence has a moral duty to accept, there is no troubled person whom one *must* help get better. But if, because of emotional or other ties, a person does wish to help a disturbed individual, then the helper must accept him, *fully* accept him.

This means that as soon as the relative or associate does something particularly stupid, pigheaded, or irritating, the helper must immediately ask himself: *"Why* did he do that?" And quickly answer himself: "Because he's neurotic. Because neurotics frequently, usually, do that sort of thing. Not because he hates me. Not because he's vicious, stupid, or ruthless. Because he's a neurotic. And neurotics commonly do vicious, stupid, ruthless things."

In other words, it is silly to respond to a disturbed person's actions as if they were all personally and specifically directed against oneself. And even when they are so directed—since neurotics, as we have previously shown, often are hostile to others—a helper must realize that these anti-you actions, being the result of neurosis, stem from anti-self feelings. Pity the neurotic for being so disturbed, for having to act in an illogical, sometimes vicious, manner. But do not *blame* him for acting thus.

Remember, always, that neurotics are *made* the way they are: are taught, by their early associates and their culture, to become neurotic. They did not *wish* to become disturbed; did not voluntarily select the path to neuroticism. The main target of their disturbances is usually themselves. Even when they harm others through being disturbed, they are virtually forced by their irrational views and motives to do this harm, and they usually do it in the process of hurting themselves.

Who, then, is to blame for an individual's being neurotic, if he himself is not responsible? His parents or grandparents, who raised him? Hardly; for they too were disturbed or ignorant, and did not know what they were doing. Is society to blame? In a way, yes—since we are all its products. Actually, though, society consists of people, and if people happen to be limited, ignorant, tradition-bound individuals who unwittingly harm themselves by constructing and perpetuating illogical laws and customs, should they rightfully be blamed for this?

Why, indeed, blame anyone? Certainly, this set of factors may cause or be responsible for that set of conditions. But will *blame* stop the set of factors from operating or prevent it from leading to a consequent set of conditions. The real question is: How can we *change* these factors and *prevent* these conditions from occurring? Why not concentrate on this question instead of on the question of who is to blame?

To repeat, the first step in helping a neurotic is to accept, fully, the fact that he is disturbed and to resist blaming him in any way for being disturbed or acting badly because of his disturbance.

Once one has faced the fact that a parent, child, sibling, mate, friend, or business associate is seriously neurotic, he must next understand what neurotics are, how they get the way they are, and how they can be helped to change. Some of the material needed for this understanding can be found in the pages of this book. Other valuable material can be found in the classical and newer works on psychoanalysis and personality theory, a selected list of which will be found in the last chapter of this volume. Read some of this material. Attend some of the lectures on personality and human behavior given by local universities or scientific groups. Keep as well informed as possible on psychological findings. The more one learns about psychology in general, and clinical psychology and psychoanalysis in particular, the better equipped he will be to understand himself and other human beings and to help others with their problems.

Self-understanding is especially important in the comprehension of the emotional quirks of others. Anything one can do to look into his own heart, discover his own neurotic leanings, and remedy his emotional blockings and irrational fears will tend to help him to help others.

Although a person may not be too seriously disturbed himself, one of the best things he can do, if he is having difficulty in helping a neurotic relative or friend, is to have some amount of psychotherapeutic consultation or aid himself. It should be remembered in this connection that although one of the main functions of therapy is to aid people in overcoming their serious difficulties, this is hardly its exclusive purpose. Another of its major goals is to show reasonably nondisturbed or mildly neurotic individuals how to understand themselves and to conquer those irrationalities which prevent them from achieving their maximum potential and from living a more creative existence.

Once a helper is ready to accept a neurotic as he is and to learn enough about dynamic psychology to understand him adequately, the next step is to give the neurotic warmth and support. It cannot be too often emphasized that neurotics get the way they are largely through lack of confidence in themselves; and, originally, they lose confidence because they feel that they are already, or are in danger of becoming, unloved, disapproved, rejected, or ignored. The main things they require to bolster their confidence are an uncritical acceptance and approval, and a vital interest taken in them by their relatives and associates.

Neurotics, alas, often do not seem to deserve any warmth and approval. Instead, they frequently go out of their way to bring on rejection and disapproval. What is more, when they are accepted, they often view with suspicion almost any kindness shown them and test out their friends by ungrateful, negative responses. Consequently, they need consistent, unvarying love, and they will continue to need it for a considerable length of time before they begin to believe that it is really being given.

This does not mean that one should shamelessly flatter disturbed people in an effort to build up their ego-strength. On the contrary, they will quickly see behind such flattery in many instances, and it will boomerang. Rather, one should bolster them intelligently, with as much truth as possible. Bring their good points to their attention; show them how they are truly effective at this or that—however inept they may be at something else.

In other words, emphasize the neurotic's assets. Do not falsely deny his failings, but try to ignore them or at least to minimize them. Keep bringing up his good points at appropriate moments: let him know when he looks especially well, when he has done a good job, when he has acted better than he thought he could.

This emphasis on a neurotic's assets need not necessarily be in words, but can also be expressed by a helper's *attitudes*. The helper should take the attitude that the neurotic is good, worthy, and achieving; he should really convince himself of this so that his confident attitude will easily and normally be communicated to the neurotic.

Above all, the helper should encourage a disturbed person to do the things he is afraid of and erroneously believes he cannot do successfully. Encourage his efforts, whatever the chances of failure may be. And when he is unsuccessful at his first attempt, show him that this is only a preliminary; that the next attempts may well succeed. Try to induce the neurotic to do things at which he is fairly certain to succeed; then point out that these successes prove he can do still other things which he has been afraid of.

Convince your neurotic relative or friend that everyone fails quite frequently and that to fail is normal. Show him that the only way human beings learn is by trial and error: therefore, failure is not only common; it is a good thing—as long as one learns by it and thereby helps himself to succeed in the future.

Sometimes it is necessary to help a neurotic lower

his level of aspiration so that he doesn't attempt things beyond his ability. Encourage him to be daring—but realistic. Discourage perfectionism, or highly unrealistic expectations.

A neurotic must also somehow be induced to see that though his success may be vitally important to him, it is in some ways not *that* important to his helper. He must be made aware of the helper's confidence in his future success, of the helper's unwavering support. And when a neurotic does not succeed, he must be reassured that he is still loved and respected just as much. He must learn, too, that he is liked for himself, for some of his fine essential qualities, rather than for being successful at this or that particular thing. One must make the neurotic understand that his successes are appreciated, but that—succeeding or failing—his helper still thinks he is a great guy.

In proving to a neurotic that one is wholeheartedly on his side, the helper must at the same time make it clear that he himself is not a weakling, and is not an easy mark to be exploited or taken advantage of. It is also important that the helper adopt an attitude of firm kindness and take care to avoid pampering and babying the disturbed person.

What is firm kindness? Just what its name implies. It means being consistently pleasant to people, but setting definite limits as to how far they may impose on one, firmly sticking to those limits. It means being able to see things from other people's frames of reference, but never entirely losing sight of one's own vital wants and interests.

Take, for example, the case of a woman married to a neurotic husband who is afraid to meet people, and therefore wants to sit home every night and never have any visitors in. The thing *not* to say is: "Now look here, Joe, you know there's nothing to be afraid of in meeting other people, and that in refusing to make friends you're being stupidly neurotic. Besides, you have no consideration for me. You never think of what *I* want to do. If you really loved me, you'd get over your silly notions and take me out regularly, or at least be pleased when I ask people in."

That kind of talk will invariably convince Joe that he is even more inadequate than he previously had thought himself to be, that his wife just does not understand him, and that she is thinking only of herself. It will, in other words, tend to make him more disturbed.

Joe's wife must come to realize that her husband's refusal to see people results from neurotic anxiety and lack of self-confidence. She should do everything possible to give him greater confidence in himself, to make him feel that he *can* get along with people. She will have to work gradually, perhaps getting him to meet only one or two exceptionally compatible people at first—preferably people she has warned about his problems so that they will act warmly toward him. Once he feels somewhat at ease with these new friends, the wife should try to help him realize that he is capable of getting along with still other people as well.

If, however, Joe still remains stubbornly neurotic about meeting people and insists that his wife stay in with him, she might say something like this: "I really understand, Joe, that you don't want to meet people right now, and I'm sure you will want to later on. But in the meantime, I'm just going crazy, being steadily cooped up like this. I, maybe because of my own pe- culiarities, have a real need for people now and then. I don't mind your not wanting them, but I can't let myself be ruled by your feelings exclusively. Now, sup- pose I stay home with you most of the time, but every once in a while go out by myself. Then, when you get over not wanting to see people, which I am sure you will, we can have a fine time going out together."

Working along these lines, one can easily stand up for his own rights in marriage and in other interper- sonal relationships and, at the same time, show an un- derstanding of other people's neuroses and avoid irri- tating them. To let a neurotic take complete charge of one, however, merely because he is neurotic, often gives the disturbed person an incentive to prolong or intensify his disturbance, for he then has an excuse for remaining a baby and, like a baby, expecting to get his own way. Moreover, the neurotic tends to lose respect for anyone who is an easy mark, and then he loses still more respect for himself for associating with such a weak, namby-pamby person.

Besides, neurotics often do not really want to get their own way. They want to be understood, accepted, loved, approved. Frequently they know they are not doing the correct thing and feel even worse because no one stops them. One of my own relatives, for example, enjoyed taking full advantage of her husband's concessions no matter how unreasonable her demands were. But when he finally let her spend all their vacation money for a trip by herself, while he stayed home in the sweltering city, she loathed him for being so weak and hated herself for taking advantage of him. These feelings served to increase her disturbance.

What neurotics need, sometimes almost more than anything else, is a good model with whom they can identify and from whom they can gain strength. This is often why they undertake psychotherapy—not merely to gain love and understanding from their therapist, but to use his strength, his personality, his non-neuroticism. I was confronted with this need when a patient who had been referred both to me and to another therapist obtained interviews with both of us and then decided to stay with me. "What made you decide against the other man and in my favor?" I asked.

"Well, it was this way," my patient replied. "I went to see him, and the first thing I noticed was that his room was literally filled with smoke. I am trying to cut down on my smoking. Then, he spoke in a low tone of voice that I could hardly hear. Finally, I saw that he weighed about 250 pounds. And, as I told you last time, I have a weight problem. Well, I said to myself, if he's so poorly disciplined in his own life, I don't see how he could possibly be of much help to me."

The stronger and less neurotic one is, the more a disturbed person is likely to trust him, to feel confident that he can be helpful. So one should be firm with neurotics. A helper will also have to decide on the limits of attention he can give to a neurotic and then be sure to adhere to these limits. But at the same time he will have to show the neurotic that he is adhering to them because they will be valuable to both of them, the helper and the helped. The neurotic must feel that the person assisting him is the strongest possible ally on whom he can depend for aid—even if not for mollycoddling. One must be kind *and* firm; not one *or* the other.

Above all, one must not permit a neurotic to blackmail him emotionally. Frequently, as in the case of a mother who suddenly acquires a heart condition or severe indigestion just when her favorite son is about to marry, a disturbed person uses sickness for blackmailing purposes. If he is able to get others to do things his way by pleading illness or acute unhappiness, he is quite likely to become a chronic sufferer and continue to exploit others unmercifully. One should never submit to this kind of blackmail in dealing with a neurotic, for he can be one of the world's worst tyrannic martyrs. Be kind; but stand firm.

One central rule in dealing with a neurotic is: *do not criticize!* As we have pointed out previously, neurotics get the way they are largely from being criticized too much by their parents or early associates. Because they have thus become oversensitized, they can take virtually no further criticism. If one gives such criticism, he will only be increasing rather than decreasing their feelings of worthlessness.

Criticism, moreover, rarely moves people to constructive action. The general problem in getting human beings to change their "poor" for "better" behavior is to induce them to go from point A to point B. But most of us, when told that we *should* move from A to B, or that we are idiots for not so moving, balk and tend to stand still or go backward. We resent being pushed or pressured even for our own good.

Neurotics, in particular, tend to be ornery and unamenable to logical appeals that take the form of overt or implied criticism. To tell them that they should, for their own good, go from point A to B is usually equivalent to saying: "Look here, you fool! You know darned well that you are harming yourself by remaining at A instead of going to B. Now why don't you stop being a dunce, and do what's good for you?" To almost anyone this will sound like censure.

Neurotics constantly blame themselves for being "crazy," for having disturbed symptoms; and if someone else blames them for these same things, this only increases their self-blame. What one must do, instead, is attack *not* them or even their behavior, but the *ideas* which lie behind their symptoms. If, for example, a neurotic friend is afraid to ride in trains, it is useless to tell him: "Oh, come on, Jim. You know how silly it is to be afraid of trains. You know that trains are perfectly safe." Certainly he knows in most instances how silly his phobia is, and that riding in trains is not, in general, dangerous. But if someone emphasizes these irrationalities, it is, in effect, like telling the neurotic that he is an idiot—which he is quite willing to believe, probably, and in believing, quite likely to become more neurotic.

The thing to do, instead, is to try to find the idea behind Jim's fear of riding in trains. Obviously, to be afraid, he must be telling himself that something is dangerous about trains. Thus, he might be telling himself that the train will crash—and that would be disastrous; or, that in a crowded train he will be forced to be in close physical contact with a man or woman—and that would be unpleasant; or, that if he were to have an attack of diarrhea in a train he might not be able to get to the bathroom in time—and that would be most embarrassing. The helper's job, if he wants to undermine Jim's phobia, is to try to discover what illogical ideas Jim is dreaming up to create his fear, and then to tackle not Jim, and not even his fear, but his irrational ideas.

Thus, if one discovers that Jim is really afraid of dying in a train crash, he could point out to Jim that very few crashes occur these days; that most of those that do occur are minor and result in few fatalities; that everyone has to die someday; that worrying about being killed in a train crash will hardly reduce his chances of getting into other accidents, such as auto crashes; that preserving one's life at the expense of continual worry is hardly worth the effort; and so on.

This type of attack on the ideological bases of a neurotic's fear will often do a lot of good. In many instances, however, just because one is intimately related to the neurotic, the latter expects certain things that he ordinarily would not expect from other people. In such cases, a helper may have to do something more to overcome the neurotic's inertia and induce him to move from point *A,* where he is being harmed, to point *B,* where he would be happier. What is this something more?

The answer, in large part, is love. Out of love for another, a person will not only move in a desired direction but will actually endure injury or even death if it would help the other. If one really convinces a neurotic—or, for that matter, a so-called normal—individual that one loves him, sees things from *his* frame of reference, is truly on his side, that neurotic will often do virtually anything for one, including, at times, surrendering some of his neurotic behavior.

To be specific, consider the problem of a man who wants to have frequent sex relations with his wife. But the wife, because of a neurotic fear of too-frequent sex activity, desires to have them once or twice a month. If the husband uses ridicule with his wife, she balks all the more. If he pleads with her, she says that she would like to have sex relations more often, but just can't feel comfortable when she does so. Impasse. The more the man ridicules or pleads, the more uncomfortable she feels, and the more hostile toward him she becomes, the more her neurosis intensifies.

The husband should try a different line. He should be most understanding of the wife's predicament and show her that he realizes she has her reasons and is not merely trying to annoy him by her sex behavior. He should also try, if possible, to discover the basic cause for her fear of sex and to show her that even though she once may have had good reasons for it, these no longer apply. He should not make fun of her sex fears or superstitions, but rather should attempt to get behind them and undermine them with different, more logical attitudes.

Above all, he must love her. Show her that in spite of his own sexual disappointment, he does not resent her. Admitting frankly that he is inconvenienced, he should try, if possible, to get her to satisfy him in noncoital ways if she is afraid of intercourse. He must be honest about his own feelings, but at the same time show her that he loves her, even though he may not love the inconveniences she causes him.

If one consistently, wholeheartedly loves a neurotic person even when he is inconveniencing or depriving one, the neurotic will begin to feel that at least one human being has true respect for and confidence in him, and will begin to lose the feelings of inadequacy and hostility which underlie his neurosis. Secondly, he will come to feel that he has a partner, a true helper, and that therefore he has a better chance to overcome his fears and disturbances. Thirdly, he will normally tend to love the helper in return, and out of this love will often begin, quite spontaneously, to do things for his helper that he would not think of doing for anyone else in the world—including, quite possibly, trying to overcome his neurotic fears that inconvenience his "partner."

Love begets love; and begotten love often begets action. Naturally, this does not work invariably, since one's spouse may be so neurotic about his sex or other impulses that even extreme love may not induce him to try to work through his neurosis. But, as psychotherapists have clearly seen since Freud's early discoveries about the nature of transference in the therapeutic relationship, insight into oneself and action to back up that insight are usually helped by a patient's positive feelings, or love, for a therapist. Similarly, in

a nontherapeutic relationship, if one can somehow induce a neurotic to love him dearly, the neurotic sometimes begins to work on his own cure.

The next important step in trying to help a neurotic
is doing something to relieve his guilt. At bottom,
virtually every neurotic is abnormally guilty—fearful
that he is doing the wrong things and that others will
therefore not like him. To relieve this guilt, two main
procedures can be used: being lenient, noncritical,
and permissive when the neurotic does something
"bad" or mistaken; and encouraging him to conform
to his own standards and generally do the things about
which he will not need to feel guilty.

Consider, first, the policy of leniency. Neurotics tend
to allow themselves little leniency in many areas. They
criticize themselves for every little wrong, and forgive themselves little or nothing. If a helper, therefore,
is permissive and forgiving, the neurotic may tend to
take over similar attitudes toward himself and begin to
be more lenient with himself.

Suppose one lives with a neurotic who feels guilty
about not loving his mother sufficiently. If the helper
acts as if it is hardly the greatest crime in the world to
have ambivalent feelings toward one's mother, the neurotic may be able to take a different attitude toward his
own lack of intense mother love. Or, taking a somewhat different approach, a helper can try to discover
why the disturbed person dislikes his mother and do

something toward helping him overcome this dislike.

In being permissive with neurotics, one's own attitudes and actions are often more important than his words. If a woman is enormously guilty about her sex activities, merely telling her not to feel guilty will hardly suffice if the helper himself has similar guilt and shows it in his behavior. Being a good model for a disturbed person is one of the most effective ways of reaching him; this is particularly true as far as unnecessary guilt is concerned.

The other approach to reducing neurotic guilt—that of discouraging disturbed people from doing the things that will make them feel guilty—seems to be directly opposed to the first approach, but actually it is not. For human beings who live in any form of society should, as we noted in the last chapter, feel that they are wrong about some of the things they do, otherwise that society would not exist very long. If no one thought is was wrong to steal, rape, or murder, everyone would try at times to get away with these acts, and chaos would result.

Although one should be permissive and forgiving with neurotics, he should not try to take away their entire sense of wrongdoing, but only their unnecessary, illogical, or exaggerated guilt. In terms of the philosophy outlined in the last chapter, one should try to induce a neurotic associate to say to himself, when he does something that is needlessly harmful to others, "I certainly did this deed, and I want to admit that I was wrong about doing it." The helper should then induce the neurotic to follow up with "All right, admitting my wrong, now let me see how I can make restitution for this deed and be sure I won't repeat it in the future," instead of, "What a terrible villain I am for committing this deed! Let me see how I can best punish myself for doing it."

In getting a neurotic to admit his mistaken or immoral behavior and to concentrate on preventing himself from repeating it in the future, one can often help him by inducing him to avoid the activities (or lack of activities) that led to his wrongdoing.

Suppose, for instance, that a man, in order to have sex relations with a woman, is lying to her in telling her that he wishes to marry her, when actually he is already married and has on desire to divorce his wife. Under these circumstances, he will often tend to feel uncomfortable—as well he might. And, usually, the most effective way of reducing his guilt is to induce him to stop lying and to accept the consequences of telling the truth, even if this means that his girl friend will refuse to have anything more to do with him.

However, one should not say to his friend in this predicament: "Look here, Jack, you're being an awful heel to treat the girl like that. Why don't you stop being a louse and tell her the truth?" Such behavior on a helper's part will probably increase the neurotic's tension, make him feel that one is against him, and encourage him to find some rationalization for his behavior.

Instead, a person who wants to help should try to reduce a neurotic's guilt by showing him that unless he does things the hard way, unless he lives a reasonably moral life, he himself will be the loser, since he will always be in conflict with his *own* views and concepts of morality, and in the long run will gain more suffering than pleasure. Or, in other words, any satisfaction gained by engaging in behavior of which one disapproves oneself is more than counterbalanced by the extremely painful feelings of guilt, self-loathing, and depression that accompany such behavior. And, in the final analysis, the satisfaction simply is not worth the pain.

Whenever a person experiences guilt, then he must be acting illogically. For feeling guilty about normal behavior is certainly illogical. And if one feels guilty about certain unapproved activities which he engages in, the illogic lies in his having participated in them when he knew their nature. If the first is the case, the neurotic should obviously change his attitude, recognize that a particular action is not really wicked, and get over feeling guilty about it. If the second is the situation, he should obviously change his behavior and thereafter refrain from engaging in the guilt-provoking activity.

Sometimes, by remaining calm oneself, by continuing to accept the guilt-ridden person, and by showing that one is interested only in reducing instead of augmenting his feeling of guilt, a neurotic can be shown either how to stop feeling irrationally guilty or how to stop doing the illogical things of which he is ashamed.

Assuming that the individual one is trying to help has done truly immoral or unwise things, one can try to help him use his guilt constructively and prophylactically rather than destructively. For if a disturbed person has made bad mistakes in his behavior, and has needlessly harmed others thereby, there still is no point in his self-condemnation. The basic purpose of acknowledging wrongdoing should be to prevent a person from repeating the wrong behavior, and it is in this direction that one can help his neurotic friends or relatives with their guilt.

Thus, if one's son has unnecessarily harmed a neighbor's child, one can show him that he has acted improperly—and that the remedy for his antisocial behavior is not for him to punish himself (or for you to punish him), but for him to resolve to be more than pleasant to the neighbor's child in the future. Or if a neurotic wife is inordinately guilty because she has not been taking care of the house properly, one can show her that such guilt will be easily quieted if she becomes a model housekeeper in the present and future.

The main objective, then, when one is dealing with

neurotic guilt, is to convince the disturbed person that he really has little to be guilty about, or if he has good reason for guilt, that he can eradicate it by constructive behavior in the present and future. If a helper can successfully implant this idea in a guilt-burdened neurotic, he may help the disturbed person considerably.

One effective way of helping a neurotic relative or friend overcome feelings of guilt and worthlessness is to reduce certain demands on him, at least temporarily. Many a troubled person, because he consumes enormous amounts of energy hating himself and others, becomes overburdened by the regular work of caring for a home, running a business, or participating in organizational activity. At these times, such an individual may display acute exhaustion, develop different kinds of physical symptoms, become extremely agitated, or even go into a severe state of depression.

If a neurotic associate begins to show symptoms like these, it is well in many instances to reduce his load. Then, while one is helping him build confidence in himself by means of some of the other methods discussed in this chapter, his full load of active responsibility can gradually be built up again.

In gauging the work load that a neurotic can realistically be expected to maintain, one should take care, while not letting him do too much, not to let him do too little, either. For work itself, especially when it is productive, can be effectively anti-neuroticizing.

Sometimes more, rather than less, activity should be prescribed for a disturbed individual, since such activity may serve to divert him from his neurotic thinking. So, although temporarily a neurotic associate may have to have his responsibilities reduced, in a few months it may be fully as important that he have them increased again. If one carefully observes a disturbed friend or relative and is able to get him to experiment to some extent with different kinds of work and different responsibility levels, he should be able to work out suitable schedules which will help the disturbed person overcome his loss of self-confidence. In deciding on a specific program for a seriously disturbed person, however, some professional consultation may also be required.

Clearly the biggest hurdle any neurotic has to overcome is that created by his irrational fears: his fear of being disapproved of and rejected for doing the wrong things; and his fear of bodily harm or of death. Sometimes, one can reason with a neurotic, show him how silly his fears are, and bring him to a rational viewpoint. In so doing, however, merely tackling the fears themselves is ineffective; instead, the irrational bases of the fears must be ferreted out and attacked.

Thus, if a neurotic friend is afraid to play tennis, little good is likely to result from merely telling him that tennis is a fine game and that it is silly to fear it. Usually he knows this already and, in fact, hates himself all the more—precisely because he does know it.

What the neurotic does not know is that he has some underlying belief that makes tennis appear hazardous to him, when it really is not a dangerous game. Thus, he may believe that it would be disastrous if he played tennis badly because people would then disapprove of him for being a poor player and their disapproval would be unbearable. Such a belief is quite illogical, since it is unlikely that people would disapprove of him if he did play tennis poorly and, even if they did, there is no good reason he could not bear such disapproval.

Rather than attack this neurotic's fears directly, it would be more effective to attack the irrational *ideas* that lie behind his fears and force him, as long as he retains such ideas, to have the fears. Such ideas, we repeat, can sometimes be undermined if a helper ferrets them out, shows the neurotic that he has them, and demonstrates how illogical they are.

One of the best ways of attacking the irrational beliefs that lead to excessive fear is to induce a neurotic to become more familiar with the thing he is afraid of. By direct contact with it, he will begin to lose his fear. It is almost impossible, in fact, for a human being to retain his fear of virtually anything when he becomes sufficiently familiar with it. High mountain peaks, bloody hand-to-hand battles, bleak ocean wastes—even these become less frightening to most people who come into close continuous contact with them. It is almost unheard of for an individual to continue to practice some activity without becoming more competent at it, and increasing competence at an activity drives away what is probably the greatest and most ubiquitous of all our fears today—fear of failure.

Fear-avoidance, moreover, reinforces or rewards fear. Running away from the things one is afraid of keeps him from becoming familiar with these things or getting practice at them; and, by temporarily reducing his anxiety, tends to make him in the long run more loath to face the thing he fears. Therefore, the neurotic is not only irrationally afraid of something; he also usually refrains from doing the thing he fears, and winds up by fearing it all the more.

A number of different techniques may be employed to help a neurotic face the things he fears. For example, a helper can serve as an excellent model by doing the feared act himself and proving to the neurotic that it is really not so frightening. Or one can go along with the neurotic and keep him company in doing something he cannot face alone, such as taking a plane ride, for instance. Occasionally one can trick a neurotic into doing some presumably awesome thing—getting him to take his first plane ride, perhaps, by pretending that there is a railway tieup and that planes are the only practical means of transportation for the moment.

More frequently, one can induce the action a neurotic fears by offering him some special incentive—paying for his vacation trip if he will take a plane instead of a train or bus. Or one can sometimes help condition a disturbed individual to a feared experience by pairing it with a non-feared or pleasant experience. The choice of paired activities would, of course, vary according to the circumstances of each individual case.

By fair means or foul, then, a helper somehow induces his neurotic associate to do and to keep doing the things he fears, and the neurotic will then usually tend to lose his fears and eventually may even enjoy the very things which frightened him. Nothing succeeds like success; if one can help a neurotic to survive contact with a feared person or thing, he will normally succeed in overcoming his negative attitude toward it.

Many years ago, before I even had the idea of becoming a psychologist, I was friendly with an exceptionally shy boy who wanted very much to be successful with girls but who rarely had the courage to ask them for dates or to make any moves toward them when he did occasionally date them. He was so backward in this respect that he would know a girl for months and never get up the courage to hold her hand or to try to kiss her good night.

I felt something should be done to help my friend but didn't know exactly what I could do. So I enlisted the aid of my own steady girl friend, a vivacious and active girl who was very sociable. She immediately tackled the problem and came up with what seemed to me to be a possible practical solution. I was to let her know whenever I expected my friend to be visiting me, and she would arrange to come over that day or evening, bringing with her one of her attractive and intelligent girl friends—fortunately, she had many of them. Then, after spending some time at my place, she would see to it that I walked home with her, leaving my friend, of course, to take the other girl home.

We tried this procedure several times and it soon began to take effect. Not only was my friend forced into seeing several girls, but my girl friend would subsequently manage to let him know that he had made a hit with this or that girl whom he had been gently coerced into taking home, and that the girl would very much like to see him again. He soon began to feel at ease while talking to these girls and, in addition, to believe that he was making a good impression on them.

After a while, my friend began to acquire an entirely different picture of himself, actually coming to view himself as something of a captivating young man. Moved by his new self-estimation to be more daring with these girls, he began to make occasional affectionate overtures and, as is usual in these cases, to be accepted in a reasonable percentage of his tries. It was not long before he was beginning to see himself as a kind of college Casanova! The whole business finally ended when he started going steadily with one of the girls. Ultimately he married her—many years, in fact, before either my girl friend or I (we eventually parted) managed to maneuver ourselves into the state of matrimony with different mates!

One of the main helps to a neurotic may result from giving him interpretations of the specific causes and reasons for the continuance of his disturbance, but this method should be used with extreme caution by amateurs. Even in the hands of a trained psychotherapist, detailed interpretations of the causes of neurosis are double-edged swords that must be handled with great care.

In making specific interpretations for a patient, a therapist generally says something like this: "Let us see, now. You say that you think your resentment toward your boss arises out of the inconsiderate way he treats you. Could it be, however, that this is not the whole story? Could it also be that, because your boss is an authority figure, and your father, too, when you were a child, was a similar kind of authority figure, you actually hate your boss, at least in part, because he resembles your father, and because you are transferring to him some of the old attitudes you had toward your father?"

Or the therapist may say: "According to the story you've told me, you seem, on the surface, to love your mother dearly and to be very sorry that you've caused her all this heartache with your delinquent behavior.

Your acts themselves, however, would seem to indicate that you do everything possible to cause her the heartache which you say you want to prevent. Could it be that, unconsciously, you really resent your mother very much, and are almost deliberately acting the way you do, because you realize that this is what would hurt her most?"

This kind of specific interpretation, relating the individual's conscious thinking and behavior to his underlying, unconscious feelings, is one of the most important aspects of intensive psychotherapy or psychoanalysis. The therapist is able to make such interpretations because he has a wide knowledge of human personality, because he knows the particular patient quite intimately, and because he is trained to select a true and useful interpretation among many false and useless alternatives. Even then, the therapist often errs interpretively, and must be prepared to confess his mistakes and rectify them with better interpretations.

Because a friendly helper is not a therapist and not highly trained to be rigorously selective about deep interpretations, and because he may often be more wrong than right in making them, he must be most careful about getting into this area of therapy when he attempts to help a neurotic. Usually, if one does make interpretations, they should be made only when good rapport has been established between the helper and his neurotic associate. And there must be no attempt to cram them willy-nilly down his throat. Interpretations, moreover, should be cautiously and effectively timed and should be made skeptically and tentatively, without dogmatism. Instead of saying, "Because you do this and think that, it is obvious that this other thing must be true," interpretations should be phrased along the lines of, "Seeing that this is so, is it possible that—" or "In view of the fact that you say and do this, could it be that you—"

Providing that a helper does not attempt to be a poor man's analyst, and providing that he is not too disturbed himself and has a good knowledge of psychodynamic principles, it is possible for him to attempt mild and cautious interpretations that may lead a neurotic relative or friend toward some insight into his own disturbance. If one sticks to general rather than specific uncoverings, he is likely to be on the safe side. Thus, as we noted previously, it is fairly safe to predict that a neurotic is telling himself that *something* is dreadful or catastrophic and that in telling himself how awful this thing is he is creating disturbed feelings and behavior. *What* the disturbed person is catastrophizing may not be easy to discover; therefore, one is on safer ground if he tries to get the neurotic himself to discover what this "terrible" thing is.

General interpretations of this sort may be especially useful with individuals who are adamant toward obtaining psychotherapeutic help. Sometimes these people may be led to accepting such aid by a helper's starting the interpretative ball rolling and then explaining that he does not have the training to go too far. But the helper must watch his step! No matter how gentle or cautious he may be in interpreting, he may tend to go too far, or the disturbed person may not be able to take it. If the neurotic grows extremely defensive and resistant, or if he becomes terribly agitated or depressed, or if his behavior becomes bizarre shortly after one has been doing some interpreting for him, it is wiser to consult a good professional psychotherapist before going any further.

A safer, though still rather hazardous, technique which may be used to help neurotics is that of giving them advice and support. Neurotics, almost by definition, are persons who frequently cannot stand on their own two feet, and who therefore come to others for advice. But what advice one should give them is often not an easy thing to determine.

In the main, it is probably best to stick to co-operative planning when trying to help a neurotic associate. That is to say, instead of merely telling him what to do and practically doing it for him, it is better to plan *with* him, and thereby give him the feeling that he himself is in the center of the support-giving process. Otherwise he may take even the best-meant advice as criticism of his own inability to solve problems; or he may accept one's support so wholeheartedly that he becomes utterly dependent on outside help and refuses to try to do anything for himself. Helping a neurotic friend with his planning, however, and giving him the idea that he is thinking and doing *with* rather than *through* one is more likely to be effective in inducing him to change his neurotic behavior.

Advice and support, like other techniques of helping a neurotic, should be well timed. The less an individual is able to function for himself, the more desirable it usually is to give him considerable support. If he is really at a low ebb, cannot work effectively by himself, has confused ideas and feelings, acts childishly, and seems to be getting into increasing difficulty, letting him be dependent for a while may do him a lot of good.

If, on the other hand, a neurotic friend seems to be largely a spoiled individual who is perfectly able to do things for himself, but would rather let other people do them for him, giving him too much support may encourage him to keep on being dependent forever. Or, if he is an individual who was once very helpless, but is now feeling stronger and is ready to take steps to help himself, too much support can again be harmful. In general, one should try to give the neurotic the degree of support and advice that he needs at a given time, but not keep on supporting and advising him largely to fulfill one's own needs for having someone dependent on him.

Several years ago I treated a girl who appeared to be exceptionally disturbed, partly as a result of having been rejected in several successive love affairs. Naturally, I tried to bolster her confidence as much as possible, and to lead her, for the time being, away from other intense emotional involvements in which she might be hurt again. Whenever she told me about some new male she had met, I would get her to find out all possible information about him, and to take his initially favorable attitudes toward her with a great deal of skepticism.

Things went quite well with her for a while, probably because she managed to avoid all harrowing involvements. But then, one day she seemed to be on the brink of the precipice again: she had met a most fascinating man and had become quickly and intensely enamored of him. For his part, he seemed to reciprocate her feelings, but I was doubtful that this could be so. He was, it appeared, an outstanding person; and I wondered how attached he was becoming to my patient, who, although herself a charming and fine girl, was so obviously disturbed.

I therefore did everything possible to get my patient to put the brakes on her feelings for this new man in her life and to question his attitudes toward her. To no avail. "I am perfectly sure," she insisted, "that I am not doing the same thing with him as I did with those other fellows. And I know that I can take care of myself this time, even if anything should go wrong."

"All right," I said, "but don't forget the risks involved."

"I'm quite willing to take them."

There was nothing more I could do; so, in spite of my misgivings, she continued with the affair. A few weeks later, my worst expectations seemed to be fulfilled. Her new boy friend was proving to be inconsistent and fickle, and she was having a difficult time discovering what his actual feelings toward her were. Much to my surprise, however, she handled the situation with unusual calmness and maturity, and not only refrained from getting hurt in the process, but so impressed her boy friend with her good sense and stability that his own doubts and indecision vanished. A few months later they were married, and to my knowledge have remained happy. This case taught me a good lesson: never to underestimate an individual's power to overcome disturbance and, once initial support and help are given, to get to the point where he or she may no longer need it.

No matter what method one uses to help a troubled person, his best bet is action rather than words, and the best kind of help is serving as a good model oneself. For a neurotic frequently learns to be the way he is by identifying with and copying the behavior of his early life models—usually his parents. If someone who has close contact with him in later life can consistently act as a better model, a neurotic will often begin to identify with that person and copy his behavior.

Learning by example, moreover, is one of the most convincing of all methods. When one is told to buy a certain stock or to shop at a particular store, he is more likely to have confidence in the advice if he finds that the person giving it is himself investing in this stock or shopping at this store. Similarly, if one remains calm in the face of difficulties, behaves in an adult manner in his vocational and social relations, and works things out in a logical instead of an irrational manner, then a neurotic is much more likely to have faith in one's views on human behavior than if that person is consistently childish, excitable, and illogical. Perhaps the most effective of all methods of helping a neurotic, therefore, is to help oneself with one's own problems, and thereby set a good example for the neurotic.

Another effective way to help a troubled person is to get him actively interested in people and things outside himself. For neurotics, because of their extreme concern over being approved by others, usually are exceptionally self-centered and not really interested in others. And because they are not basically interested in others, people quickly note this and in turn are not interested in them. This leads neurotics to hate themselves more, especially when they finally come to realize that they do not really care for anyone. Then they become additionally guilty about their inability to love.

Getting a neurotic vitally interested in things and people outside himself has several distinct advantages. It distracts him from his own worries, gives him worthwhile goals to live for, makes it possible for him to succeed at some venture, and frequently provides him with interesting companions who serve as good models.

If, then, one can encourage a neurotic relative or friend to participate in outside ventures and become involved with other human beings, one may appreciably help him surmount his disturbances. Realistically, of course, one should not push him into overly difficult tasks or into relationships with people who are bound to reject him and make him more disturbed. But usually some interest or some individuals with whom he can make profitable contact can be found.

The best interests, in this connection, are those that are vitally absorbing, and the most absorbing interests are usually creative. If one can get a disturbed person occupied with writing rather than merely seeing plays, or with painting canvases rather than collecting them, or with other actively creative pursuits, he will have a better chance of getting him thoroughly absorbed in something besides his neurotic problems.

Best of all, in some instances, is to arouse in a neurotic a genuine interest in other people. Neurosis, basically, is a social disease, since it arises when a person feels inadequate, assumes that he appears that way to others, and therefore becomes self-hating and hostile. And the best antidote to desperately wanting the love and approval of others is to love those others oneself. Such action will, in most instances, not only encourage others to love one in return; better still, it will often make one relatively unconcerned about whether they do or not.

Being loved by others is pleasant enough; but it is a minor gain compared to the ability to love others actively and creatively oneself. Being loved is a passive occupation that easily palls and bores, but loving is a vitally absorbing, active expression of oneself, a creative manifestation of the interaction between one's inner urgings and strivings and one's environment. Loving, or being creatively absorbed in, something outside oneself, moreover, is the basic solution to the problem of neurotic self-centeredness. For, by being truly concerned with loving and helping someone else grow and develop, one may acquire an authentic sense of personal accomplishment, have little time to worry about himself, learn significant things about the state of his own feelings that he might never otherwise learn, and have emotional experiences invaluable to his own growth.

When I was working at a mental institution several years ago, the director came to see me one day to discuss the problem of one of the Gray Ladies, or volunteer helpers, attached to the institution. This woman was a high-strung, obviously disturbed person whom the director had had misgivings about taking on, but whom he had finally accepted because she got along so well with some of the other Gray Ladies.

Once on the staff, she did her work well, and all the inmates of the institution with whom she came into contact were very fond of her. That was the trouble, the director said: she did so much for these inmates, even to the extent of corresponding with them long after they left the institution, that some of the professional staff were beginning to wonder if unhealthy relationships were not being set up.

I could not see any great harm resulting from these relationships; and I could see that, on both sides, they might lead to some real good, since the woman and the inmates both needed warm emotional attachments. I recommended, therefore, that nothing be done about this woman and that she be permitted to remain a member of the volunteer group.

Fortunately, I guessed right in this case. Not only did the woman continue to be one of the best volunteer workers at the institution, but she gained so much by being able to devote herself to helping others that she became considerably less disturbed herself. Although she had had exceptionally low ego-strength when she first began her institutional work, she made such rapid strides in gaining self-confidence that even the nonprofessional workers at the institution began to notice and comment on her improvement.

After a few more months, she was doing so well that, at the director's suggestion, she began to think of making a career of social work; and, in spite of the fact that she was forty-five years of age at the time, she went back to school and eventually became a competent and successful social worker. Although she never obtained any direct treatment herself, the indirect psychotherapy she obtained through becoming interested in, and devoting her time and energies to, others was immensely important in helping her overcome some of her own serious problems.

Encouraging a neurotic relative or associate to develop an interest in others is, therefore, doing him the best possible of good turns. But it may be difficult to bring about, for the neurotic's fear of being unloved or unaccepted usually prevents him from building relationships with others. In such cases, there are several ways one can help a neurotic to break down his emotional block:

• To make sure that the neurotic meets new and interesting people, introduce him to some of one's own friends, take him to parties and gatherings, or get him to join social groups that one belongs to oneself. Speak favorably of the people he is to meet until finally he begins to want to meet them.

• It will help a troubled person to get along better with the people he meets if someone he trusts were to show him that these people are not really against him, as a neurotic often thinks people are, but that they are eager to be friendly. It is also important that the neurotic be helped to realize other people have problems too, and to see that these others may be troubled. He must learn that others are interested in him and that certain values can be achieved by maintaining contacts with others.

• A neurotic's interest in others must be kept from flagging when he suffers a temporary setback in a relationship. He will benefit, then, from having someone explain why a particular person does not like him and show him what can be done about it. When a neurotic is helped to understand the disturbances of other people, he learns not to take the negative attitudes of these others too seriously. If he can be encouraged to develop the habit of being with others, in time his friendships may catch fire and develop into something worth while. But he will still need additional support from his helper when his relationships with others are not going too well; then a helper has to be careful that the neurotic does not become too completely dependent, but retains some outside contacts as well.

In several important ways, then, a disturbed person can be encouraged to initiate and maintain intimate contacts with other people, and thereby fulfill himself creatively as a social being. And, in so doing, one may succeed not merely in turning him away from being too self-centered, but in inducing him to build affectionate relations with others that will truly minimize his neurotic needs.

Besides the methods for helping a neurotic outlined in this chapter, there is one additional resource to which a helper will sometimes have to turn—getting a neurotic friend or relative to seek professional help when that is necessary. Disturbed people are not easy to help, and frequently they have constructed important barriers against letting a friend or anyone at all help them. Even when they recognize the depth of their neuroses, they frequently feel that they are so far gone, so hopeless, that there is no use in doing anything about the situation and, despite all urging, they will not even try to get better. In such instances, they invariably need intensive psychotherapy.

To complicate matters still more, overcoming a neurotic's refusal to accept therapy often is a far from easy task. The disturbed person will say, for example, that professional help is too expensive; or he has no time for it; or he knows someone who was not helped by it; or he is afraid of being psychologically torn apart and not being put back together again; and so on. How, then, can a reluctant neurotic be induced to accept psychotherapy?

Not, certainly, by nagging. Explaining the virtues of psychotherapy and affirming one's own belief in it will help convince him. But keeping after the neurotic too much is unlikely to achieve the desired result.

One must first convince a neurotic that one is on his side, wants to help him as much as possible, but is possessed of only limited ability to help. Then one can go on to the next step of reasoning and point out to the neurotic that the ability of a competent therapist is far lass limited, and that therefore professional help has certain distinct advantages. However, one should be careful not to mislead the neurotic into expecting miracles.

If possible, the neurotic should be introduced to people who have had therapy and have been considerably helped by it. Or, if one knows a good therapist socially, one should try to arrange for the neurotic to meet this individual socially so that he can see for himself what a representative of the profession looks and sounds like.

One should introduce the neurotic he is helping to reasonably sophisticated, educated people who realize the value of psychotherapy. If a disturbed person is familiar only with relatively uneducated, defensive individuals—many of whom are themselves refugees from therapy—he will keep hearing the old bromide that only "crazy" people go to see therapists, and he will be loath to do so himself. One should try, instead, to impress him with the fact that most therapy patients are not at all "crazy" but are simply people who have unusual difficulties in living their lives.

If a helper has himself had some psychotherapeutic

aid, he should tell his neurotic friend about this fact, and show him exactly how he was benefited. If the neurotic then shows interest, it may sometimes be advisable for the helper to see the psychologist or psychiatrist first and explain the neurotic's situation to him, especially regarding reluctance to undertake treatment. Then, when the therapist finally sees the disturbed person, he may be better prepared to overcome the latter's doubts and get him to enter a full-scale therapeutic relationship.

Occasionally, a neurotic can be half-tricked into starting therapy. This is particularly true of someone who really would like to have professional treatment but just cannot bring himself to take the first step. Under these circumstances, it is helpful to use some kind of ruse to get him into a therapist's office, if just for a single visit. Many of my own patients, for example, are induced to see me first for the purpose of discussing someone else's problem—that of a wife, sister, parent, or child. In this manner, they become acquainted with the therapist, are able to get some indication of his ability to help people, and are frequently led to discuss their own serious problems and to begin a therapeutic relationship.

I had an experience of this kind when I saw a man whose wife was, according to his story, terribly disturbed but would under no circumstances consider getting therapeutic help. For several sessions the husband and I discussed how we might possibly get his wife to see me; but whatever suggestions I offered he always discounted, fearing that they were not subtle enough, that his wife would see through them, and that she would absolutely refuse to come.

Finally, I suggested that he tell his wife that he was worried about their seven-year-old daughter, whose behavior was something of a problem, that he himself had not been able to give me too accurate a picture of the daughter's trouble, and that therefore I would like to see the wife to discuss the daughter's difficulties. He thought this was a fine and workable suggestion.

As he predicted, the wife immediately made an appointment to discuss the daughter with me. But she had no sooner entered my office than she began talking about her own difficulties, especially those with her husband; and, within fifteen minutes of greeting me, she had fully agreed that she herself needed treatment —and that, in fact, it was more important that she get it than that I continue to see her husband. By the time this first session ended, we had set up a schedule of future visits on a more intensive basis than that on which I was seeing the husband. He, when he learned of the results of my talk with his wife, was so astounded that he thought that I had hypnotized her or used some other dramatic technique for winning her over. Actually, I had done nothing but listen sympathetically to her complaints and show her that the only possible way she could really get to the root of her own disturbance would be by regular psychotherapeutic treatment.

This does not mean that people who are solidly opposed to psychotherapy should routinely be tricked into it. Generally, such a method will do little good, because unless an individual wants to be helped, there is little help that he will accept. But innumerable neurotics, instead of being solidly opposed to therapy, are quite ambivalent about it: they both want it and fear it. Many of these, by having some initial contact with a competent psychologist, can easily be induced to prolong that contact.

Can those who do not want therapeutic aid sometimes be forced to accept it with good results? The answer, surprisingly enough, is yes—sometimes. I have had patients who were sent to me by the courts after they had committed some sexual offense; and, although at first they came only because they were forced to come, later they developed into willing and eager patients and made considerable therapeutic progress.

I have also had patients who came to see me for only one reason: the absolute insistence of their husbands or wives. Most of these patients proved to be exceptionally difficult and many left therapy after only a few sessions, with very little accomplished. But some of them, occasionally to my own surprise, went through an initial period of resistance and then settled down to be among my hardest-working patients.

As a last resort, when it is fairly certain that no other tactic will work, it is sometimes desirable to give a neurotic friend or relative a clear-cut ultimatum and tell him that unless he accepts professional therapeutic aid, he can no longer expect one's help and support, or perhaps even one's continued association with him. Normally this procedure is not advisable, but in a few cases it is the only thing that will work.

On the whole, as we have emphasized throughout this chapter, helping a neurotic oneself, or helping him to get help, is often a most difficult task. But if one really cares for a disturbed person, and wants, for his own sake as well as the neurotic's, to help him overcome his emotional disturbance, the task can be one of the most rewarding a person will ever undertake. By all means, then, give a neurotic friend or relative a chance. There is little to lose, and often considerable to gain.

6

HOW TO LIVE WITH A PERSON WHO REMAINS EMOTIONALLY DISTURBED

Probably no neurotics are hopeless. Theoretically, virtually all of them can be considerably improved—*if* they will work hard enough for their own improvement and get sufficient help while they are working. But many of them, for one reason or another, will not try to overcome their disturbance.

Sometimes they are too old and tired to make the effort. Sometimes they will not do anything now, although they may be expected to do something in the future. Sometimes the neurotic process has gone so far that they no longer have an incentive to change. Sometimes they have been beaten down so thoroughly by life that they have little ego structure or self-confidence left with which to fight for a change. Sometimes they are morbidly afraid of any change, including getting better. Sometimes they are moderately well adjusted to their disturbance and do not want to change.

Perhaps all neurotics can get better, but many of them, temporarily or permanently, will not. To believe otherwise would be unrealistic. Even intensive psychotherapy with an excellent psychologist or psychiatrist will not benefit some neurotics to any appreciable extent, since they may for various reasons resist gaining insight or using it.

Suppose, then, that one is living or associating with a seriously disturbed individual who simply will not accept help from anyone to overcome his disturbance. Suppose that the disturbed person is one's wife, or mother, or business partner, whom he may dearly love or have good reason for maintaining intimate contact with, although the person is distinctly neurotic and very likely will remain so for the present. How, under these circumstances, can one live with this disturbed individual without becoming disturbed himself or living in perpetual terror or despair? Let us examine some of the important techniques which can be used successfully in such a case.

To live comfortably with a serious neurotic, one must first fully, unequivocally, accept the fact that he is disturbed and that disturbed people act in a distinctly aberrated manner. I have chosen the words *fully* and *unequivocally* very carefully.

This may seem, at first, to be an unimportant point. Actually, it is most important. "Of course," people tell me all the time, "I know that So-and-So is neurotic. I've known it for years. Naturally I make allowances for his disturbance."

But this is usually untrue. These people *think* they know So-and-So is neurotic; they *vaguely* know it. Actually and profoundly, however, they do not. And that makes all the difference in the world—the difference between being vaguely aware that an individual is neurotic and *truly* knowing that he is.

Consider an example. One of my friends went with a girl for two years, kept telling me how disturbed she was before he married her, but then married her anyway because he wanted an interesting, intellectually alive companion. A few weeks after the marriage, he came to me and complained bitterly: "She doesn't do a thing. She doesn't read, she doesn't want to discuss anything interesting, she doesn't want to go visiting. She just sits on her behind all day and does nothing. How can I live with a woman like that?"

"But what do you expect," I asked, "from a serious neurotic?"

"Oh, I realize she's neurotic, but—" And off he went again into another tirade.

This man, however, did not *fully* realize that his

wife was disturbed. If he had, he would have expected her to act in disturbed ways: to do exactly the kind of things she was doing. Obviously, he expected nothing of the sort and was unpleasantly surprised when she acted neurotically. Therefore, he could not possibly have been fully and unequivocally conscious of the fact that she was seriously neurotic. He said that he was; he thought he was; but he was not. And it took me several weeks to convince him that his wife was neurotic and that he should therefore expect her to act like a neurotic.

It is all important, if one is to live peacefully with a disturbed person, that one expect him to act like a neurotic. If one expects a troubled individual to act like a perfectly sane, rational, "normal" person, he is doomed to disappointment. And he will constantly be having his hopes fruitlessly raised—then viciously dashed. No one, I trust, expects an infant to act like a grownup, a professor to act like a Bowery bum. Why, then, should anyone expect a neurotic to act like a well-adjusted, mature individual?

Let us go over this once again—for it is probably *the* most important rule for living comfortably with neurotics. One must absolutely, positively, unreservedly accept a disturbed person for what he is, and expect him to act accordingly. One must not expect him to be stable, sane, rational, logical, well-behaved, sober, mature, reliable, steady, hard-working, or anything else that one expects (and often fails to find) in non-neu-rotics. Sometimes, especially for short periods, a neu-rotic may behave in a completely consistent, sound manner. But one should not be fooled! The neurotic cannot, will not, keep this up indefinitely. If he could and did, he would not be neurotic.

Not accepting a neurotic for what he is, in effect, is blaming him for his neurosis. And this, of course, will tend to make him even more disturbed since, as we have consistently said in this book, neurosis largely springs from the criticisms of others which the neurotic internalizes and turns against himself.

Blame is not necessarily expressed in the direct form of criticism, but may be indirectly shown by many kinds of attitudes and gestures. One of the chief of these is excitement or being upset. Thus, while many "normal" individuals do not overtly criticize their neurotic associates, they do become unduly excited or upset about their neurotic behavior. They show in manner, if not in words, that they think it is "awful" or "terrible" for disturbed people to be acting in a dis-turbed manner. Sensing this, the disturbed individuals often become more neurotic.

Perhaps half the misery, the disappointment, in to-day's world may be attributable to the fact that there are so many neurotics behaving in a typically disturbed manner, and so many other people who utterly refuse to accept this disturbed behavior. If only all of us—

neurotic and normal—would be sufficiently realistic to accept the fact that neurotics act neurotically, everyone would automatically be less excited, less upset, less disappointed, when people act "wrongly."

All right! So Jones gets drunk every night and he is noisy; so Smith snubs us on the street; so Mrs. Henry spies on all her neighbor's activities. What should one expect neurotics like Jones, Smith, and Mrs. Henry to do—be sober, nice, and nonsuspicious? He might just as well expect black to be white or a Dodger fan to root for the Giants.

The important thing, in accepting a neurotic the way he is, is not to *personalize* his behavior toward oneself. Naturally, as a result of his disturbance, he will sometimes act in a negative manner. But, just as often as not, he is not personally against a particular individual but is impersonally treating one just as he treats most other people—and, frequently, just as he treats himself. He may seem, by his actions, to be vicious or stupid. Actually, he is merely neurotic and, because of his neurosis, is driven to do vicious or stupid things.

Even when a neurotic deliberately goes out of his way to combat or harm someone, it is not correct to assume that he is personally against that individual. At bottom, he is still personally against himself, and is driven by his self-hatred to hate others, including perhaps the closest of friends or relatives. A man who is panic-stricken when caught in a fire will ruthlessly knock down others in order to escape. But this does not mean that he hates these others in particular, or wishes them any harm. Similarly, a neurotic frequently is quite indifferent, sometimes even friendly, to a person even while he is panic-strickenly pushing that person out of his way. It is not that he necessarily *wants* to do so; he is literally forced to be antagonistic, and he himself often regrets this.

A person is much better off in his relationships with a disturbed individual if he can learn to accept the neurotic and his acts on the level on which these acts are actually committed. If one refrains from personalizing, from thinking that the neurotic is specifically out to destroy one, and tries instead to see the disturbed person in his own tragic light, one can immeasurably help both the neurotic and himself.

One should be kind to oneself and to an emotionally disturbed associate; accept, with no reservations whatsoever, the fact that a neurotic is a neurotic. Once a person has accepted this fact, he may, if he wishes, try to get away from a disturbed relative or friend. But if he does not want to, or for some reason cannot, get away, then he must accept the disturbed behavior at its true neurotic level and adjust himself to it on that level.

An illustration I frequently give my patients is this: Suppose that you are living with a neurotic whose habit it is to get up every morning at 3 A.M. and start beating a set of kettledrums. This habit, to say the least, disrupts your sleep, and you want to do something about the matter. What can you do?

The first thing to do, obviously, is to accept the fact that the neurotic's drum-beating habits are part of his disturbance. It is unlikely that he beats the drums because he is against you, is plotting your death by physical exhaustion, or anything like that. He just has an irrepressible urge which he cannot block. Accept the fact that he has this urge. Don't get angry. Remember that, in a way, this drum-beating harms him more than it harms you. It's *his* neurosis. Don't personalize it. Tell yourself, truthfully, that you're suffering because of his disturbance—but you're suffering because he's neurotic, not because he's necessarily against you.

So keep cool. Things are bad enough at 3 A.M. without your trying to raise your own blood pressure and to commit murder. Keep telling yourself, over and over, if necessary, that your friend is emotionally disturbed. Really convince yourself of this. And, because you convince yourself, remain calm. Once you are calm, the question of what to do about the situation must be faced.

The best thing, very frankly, might well be for one of you—you or this neurotic—to move to another house. (If a person must have neurotic symptoms, we at least have the right to ask that they be reasonable ones—if we are to live with him.) That is, if you find that you cannot easily survive under the existing circumstances, by all means arrange to part company with your neurotic friend. Don't become angry with him; don't blame him for being as disturbed as he is. But calmly, self-protectively, arrange for one of you to vacate the premises.

However, if the neurotic is closely related to you and you *can't* live apart from him, the next best thing might be to rearrange your living conditions so that you are not particularly inconvenienced by his symptoms. You can, for example, insist that he get a night job, so that he can beat the drums only during the day—when you, perhaps, are out working. Or you can insist that he pay to have his room soundproofed. Or you can make some other arrangement that will let him keep his neurosis while you retain your peace of mind. The main thing, however, is to remain calm and undisturbed, for you can more effectively plan to control the situation when you are not upset yourself.

To pursue the problem, suppose that you cannot stop your friend from beating his drums in the middle of the night and, for some reason, you don't want to change the living arrangements. Then it is more important than ever that you understand his neurosis and refuse to let yourself be angered by it. His keeping you awake nights is bad enough; it is much worse if you keep yourself still more awake by hating him.

Accept his neurosis and its inconveniences. Tell yourself over and over that he cannot for the present help being the way he is; that this is the penalty (yours and his) for having been raised to become neurotic; that you live under poor conditions, and they're going to remain that way until he becomes less neurotic or you manage to contain his neurosis or to get away from him.

Tell yourself that things could, after all, be worse. Instead of beating drums, he might be beating you. Or he might beat the drums all night instead of merely for an hour or two. Or he might develop different but worse neurotic symptoms. So, if you have to keep living with this disturbed person, by all means stop pitying yourself and stop feeling that life is unjust. Because of his neurosis, things are bad. But are they really *that* bad? And will getting angry about them make things any better? On the contrary, it will doubtless make them worse.

Remain calm. Accept your friend's neurosis for what it is—an emotional disturbance. Don't try to fool yourself into believing that it is good and beneficial. But, at the same time, don't exaggerate its horrors. Accept it fully, calmly; then, at least, there will be a possibility that something can eventually be done about it.

One of the best ways to accept fully, and to avoid being unnecessarily perturbed by, the neuroses of your intimate is to employ every bit of understanding of neuroticism that you may acquire. If you truly understand what a neurotic is, and keep reminding yourself of *why* he acts the way he does, it will be almost impossible for you to become too unhappy over his behavior.

Here is another illustration I often give my clients: Suppose you walk down the street and a friend of yours leans out of a window and starts calling you all kinds of evil names. Would you be hurt by his behavior? Normally, you certainly would.

But if this same friend were leaning out of the window of a mental hospital and calling you exactly the same names, would you *then* be as severely hurt by his name-calling? Certainly not.

Why? Why in the one instance would you be quite sensitive, and in the other not? Because, obviously, you are making allowances for the friend who leans out of the mental hospital window. You *understand* that he is seriously disturbed and that his name-calling results from his disturbance rather than from his actual estimate of you or from anything you may have done. You tell yourself, in this latter instance, "Poor fellow. He's very sick, and that is why he's acting this way. When he's better again, he won't be calling me those names."

The more you understand that an individual is neurotic and that his condition explains his actions, the less likely you are to be seriously upset by his behavior. By utilizing your understanding of neurosis,

you automatically start making allowances for the annoying behavior of your associate and become less upset about it. Instead of building it up in your mind, as you would otherwise tend to do, you unconsciously start toning it down. You even become intrigued, at times, with figuring out just *why* a disturbed friend acts in some particular neurotic manner toward you; and, being so intrigued, you cannot possibly blame him or pity yourself.

Understanding breeds peace of mind. Primitive man, who understood little about nature, was probably terrified by things like eclipses, thunderstorms, and forest fires. We, because we understand these phenomena much better, are less terrified of them. Similarly, if one does not understand why a neurotic is acting in a certain manner, he will be perplexed and anxious about the neurotic's behavior. But if one does understand the whys of such behavior, he will tend to be less perplexed and anxious. And even though one does not like a neurotic's behavior, greater understanding gives him a greater degree of equanimity in facing it.

The basis for dealing with intractable neurotics lies in using to the full one's own understanding of emotional disturbance. One should learn as much about neurosis as he can and then *use* this knowledge by continually reminding oneself: "This is a neurotic with whom I am having a relationship. He acts this way

[180]

because of his disturbance—which was caused by significant factors in his early upbringing for which he is not to blame. Let me, therefore, not take his neurosis too seriously or think it is personally directed against me. He is being forced, by inner conflicts and anxieties, to act the way he does. Let me see if I can understand exactly what some of his underlying feelings are; then, even if I can't help him, I will feel more comfortable myself."

When, for the moment, a troubled person refuses to allow himself to be helped and continues to act in peculiar ways, some degree of emotional withdrawal from him may be the only feasible way one can live comfortably with him.

Take the case of one of my patients, a nineteen-year-old boy. Although he was bright, well-behaved, and talented, his parents criticized everything he did. They were members of a small sect and felt that he should live strictly in accordance with the ideals of this sect—which were totally different from the ideals of his friends and fellow college students. His parents expected him to have virtually no social life, to devote himself continually to politico-economic study, and to refrain from all sexual participation. His own inclinations were to go out with girls and to be a popular member of his group of male friends, none of whom believed in his parents' ideals.

In consequence, his parents criticized him still more

severely, called him a bum and a loafer, said that he was immoral, and predicted he would never amount to anything. I saw both parents and tried to persuade them to moderate their criticism. To no avail. As soon as they realized I was not too enthusiastically in favor of their particular ideals, they began to think that I, too, was a bum and a loafer, and could not possibly help them and their son

The only thing I could do under the circumstances —for the boy was becoming sicker by the day and could easily have ended in a mental hospital—was to induce the son to withdraw emotionally from the parents. I tried, at first, to get him to understand how disturbed his parents were, and to realize that their criticism stemmed from their own feelings of inadequacy. I tried to inure him to their criticism: to get him to predict, in advance, what they would say when he came home from a party or dance, and to avoid feeling upset by it. I showed him how they thought they were doing their best for him; but how, because of their own neuroses, they were actually trying to get him to do everything *they* wanted, without really considering *his* desires, goals, and ideals.

Gradually, this boy was able to pull away emotionally from his parents: to become little dependent on them; to care less what they thought of his behavior; to understand how sick they were. The same disagreements and arguments continued at home, but now they did not affect him—he no longer entered into the spirit of them. Finally, when he could remain undisturbed by anything his parents said, he was able to get a job and move out of the house. He saw his folks regularly and got along with them better than before. He even loved them in a quiet manner. But their emotional pull on him had vanished, and he began, for the first time, truly to live his own life instead of merely rebelling against the kind of life they wanted him to lead.

Is it justifiable for an individual to withdraw emotionally from people he may love—his parents, for instance—in order to live more comfortably with himself? It is not only justifiable, but at times imperative. For to love a hopeless neurotic unreservedly, devotedly, and dependently is to take one's emotional life in one's hands. There are many kinds and degrees of love. There is mature love and immature love: obsessive-compulsive and calm love; possessive and permissive love. If one loves a neurotic in a mature, quiet, permissive manner—nondependently and with some degree of guardedness—he will be in a better position to help the one he loves, and to maintain a healthier relationship for him and for oneself.

Consider still another of my cases. The daughter, in this instance, was attached to her father with violent ambivalence: one day she hated him wildly and the next day was utterly devoted to him. He was a psychotic individual who had been in several mental hospitals but had never appreciably improved for more than a few weeks at a time. He would upset his daughter each time by telling her that she was responsible for his having been sent back to the hospital, and that if she really loved him she would take him to live with her and her family. There was no question in my mind, when I first saw the daughter, that several more months of such emotional pressure would make her a prime candidate for a mental hospital herself.

The only step, since there was nothing to be done to help the father, was to prevent the daughter from being emotionally affected by him. This I managed to do by getting her, for the first time, fully to accept his disturbance; to see that it was no fault of hers that he was as sick as he was; and to realize how futile it was to continue to be subservient to him.

As she gradually realized all this, and became less affected by him, she changed remarkably. Her life became more efficient and organized; she was a warmer, easier-going mother; her relations with her husband improved considerably; and for the first time in many years she began to enjoy life. When her father would call, she listened to him patiently, but was not moved by anything he said. When he took turns for the worse, she was well prepared. When he returned to the mental hospital, she did not feel guilty or unduly upset. She fully understood that he was seriously sick and that, since he did not want to be helped, there was little or nothing that she or anyone else could do for him.

This is the action one must sometimes take when confronted in his intimate life with an individual who obviously is disturbed and is going to remain disturbed: one must withdraw emotionally. Understanding clearly that such a person is sick and not in any way to be blamed for being sick, one still must not, under any circumstances, let the disturbed person suck one into his sickness. Love a disturbed person—yes, but in a toned-down, somewhat cautious manner. One should not sacrifice oneself utterly nor try to be a Florence Nightingale.

In other words, no one should let himself be emotionally exploited by seriously neurotic or psychotic relatives or friends. Instead, one should keep some kind of emotional distance from them and retain some perspective in his attachments to them. Charming, fine, brilliant people they may be. But because of their neurotic limitations, they are also generally impoverished in their love relationships. They can give another person just so much, because they are utterly self-centered. If one gives to them without reservation, they frequently are unable to return that love in kind.

If, however, the neurotic one loves is salvageable, that's another story. If there is a good chance that he or she will overcome his disturbance and eventually be capable of giving more love, then by all means one should give generously of himself to help this person. But if a neurotic is practically hopeless, if he or she refuses flatly to try to get better, then one must beware. Out of self-protection, one may simply have to withdraw some of his affection or, if necessary, break off the entire relationship.

Usually this more drastic action will not be necessary. Even hopeless neurotics, as a rule, have some capacity for warm human relationships, and one can consequently have limited love involvements with them. But one must recognize the limitations, not delude himself into thinking that neurotics can love anyone profoundly, as a non-neurotic can. Unless a person relishes unrequited love, he has to be somewhat reserved and open-eyed in relationships with disturbed people. And if such relationships get too bad, it is wiser to make a strategic retreat. One must think of his own skin, for he can be sure that a neurotic intimate will have *no* regard for it.

Sometimes it is impossible, emotionally or literally, to get away from someone whose behavior is severely neurotic. What can one do in order to live comfortably with such a person?

The best procedure is to acquire a more realistic, more stoical philosophy of life. One can use his head, rather than his heart, in overcoming virtually any difficulty—including those that arise in attempting to live with a hopeless neurotic.

A rational, realistic philosophy of life includes several sane assumptions, the first of which is that the world is the way it is, and there is no point in crying or getting too angry about the way it is. This premise in no sense implies that when things are not going the way one wants them to go, he should not try to change them. Of course one should. But when things are partly or wholly unchangeable—as on many occasions they are—there is no point in getting overexcited about their unchangeability.

The frame of reference in which many so-called adults in our society see things appears to require that the world should be the way one wants it to be; that the world owes one a living; that when things do not suit a person and the world is not coming across with the living it owes him, then there is no justice and the world is no darned good. The frame of reference of a real adult is built on quite different ideas: that the present world is doubtless not the best of all possible worlds, and is certainly replete with unfairness and injustice; that it would be more agreeable if this were *not* so; but that since it is so, the wisest thing to do is to acknowledge it and stop belaboring the point.

The man with a rational attitude recognizes that the main purpose of life is living: experiencing, seeing, doing, feeling, existing. The only intelligent thing to do is to make the most of the seventy-odd years that most of us have by living them to the hilt: experiencing as many vitally interesting things as possible; taking various risks in order to gain certain pleasures; making clear-cut goals and plans and working persistently to achieve them.

The purpose of one's life may be, if one wishes it so, to make the world a little bit better than it was when he came into it: to help reorganize it in such a manner that more people have more leeway to live satisfactorily for their life span in the way they most enjoy. One can, in other words, work for a "better" or "more peaceful" or "more just" world, in which one-self and other human beings can live more happily, less neurotically.

But working for a better world should not be equated with being sadly disappointed because it does not presently exist. The existing world, which we inherited from our parents and are still modifying, is in many respects not a good, peaceful, or just one. It is full of money-grubbers, idiots, tyrants, psychopaths, and neu-rotics. And quite likely it will continue to be for some time to come.

Moreover, aside from the current unsatisfactory state of the world, man himself is a highly imperfect animal. He is more ignorant, inefficient, and nervously and physically limited than he usually cares to admit. It takes him considerable time to unlearn bad habits and learn more appropriate ones. He forgets things easily. He tends to let his emotions get in the way of his rational thinking. He has to spend up to a third of his life sleeping. He is heir to innumerable diseases and ailments. He frequently become addicted to health- and ego-destroying liquor and drugs. And these basic limitations of human beings, like the inadequacies of the cultures which humans construct, are likely to be with us for a long, long time; some of them, perhaps, forever.

The only sane philosophic attitude to take, there- fore, is a realistic one. An objective individual accepts the world and himself the way they are, not as they are supposed to be. If he doesn't like them the way they are, he tries to change them. If he can't change them, he stops trying and accepts them. He doesn't give up living because life is not what he would like it to be; he gives up crying about the way he should like it to be.

As the philosopher Epictetus pointed out almost two thousand years ago, the one thing over which we have practically no control is the activities of others. Why, then, should we always be vainly trying to control them?

Similarly, if one lives with a hopeless neurotic, he must be realistic. He must not, as we have stressed repeatedly, expect a neurotic to behave other than neurotically. And he should not keep telling himself how unfair it is that the neurotic is not different. It is not unfair. It is not fair *or* unfair. It just is. He does not have to like him; merely accept him. For what else can he do? He cannot, as we have been explaining, change this particular neurotic for the present. Nor can he, probably, stop the neurotic from doing annoying things; such conduct is characteristic of disturbed people.

What one can control under these circumstances is his own reactions, his own feelings of annoyance. Not that one can completely avoid being annoyed when someone does something he abhors. But one can work on his own feeling of annoyance and attempt to tone it down, make it more bearable. He can expect an annoying event, for instance, and tell himself it will surely come. He can ask himself how annoying it really is when it does come: watch himself—literally—being annoyed by being annoyed. Then he can show himself how foolish it is to let being annoyed annoy him. One can often get rid of some of the annoyance he thus causes himself; he can cut down, as it were, on the surplus annoyance. The main thing is not to waste your effort in trying to change a hopeless neurotic who annoys you—but instead to change your own attitudes toward him and his annoyances.

Virtually all annoyances can be appreciably reduced by taking a rational or realistic attitude toward them. Most such annoyances, when analyzed, turn out to be mere verbalizations, a matter of words. A person gets annoyed because someone has called him an evil name, or has otherwise expressed disapproval. Actually, however, it is not the words or expressions which hurt—

for how can a word, in itself, hurt?—but one's attitudes toward these words or expressions. If he *thinks* it is disastrous or calamitous to be called this name or shown that kind of disapproval, because he *thinks* so, he makes it so. When a person starts thinking differently—realizes that mere words or expressions cannot, in themselves, hurt; recognizes that because of their source—an emotionally disturbed person—the words are devoid of their usual meaning; that only physical violence can really hurt—then he can get rid of virtually all verbal vulnerability and quickly do away with most of his unhappiness.

As for the other kinds of annoyances in life, the actual physical ones—such as the painful sound of the drums at 3 A.M. or the real hurt of being struck on the head—even these can be minimized by taking realistic attitudes toward them. For, if one takes the attitude that physical hurts are to some extent inevitable in life; that dwelling on them only serves to keep in mind how painful they are; that worse things might happen; that sometimes physical ailments have certain advantages; and that the best thing, usually, is to ignore and try to forget the hurt (after presumably having taken all possible measures, such as aspirin or liniment, to reduce it), he will at least avoid exaggerating or augmenting physical hurts even though he cannot eliminate physical pain. Any other attitude is almost certain to make him feel worse.

Moreover, steps can often be taken to prevent the recurrence of physical ills. If one has frequent headaches, he can see a physician, learn the cause of the headaches, and usually do something to eliminate it. If he is physically injured by someone, he can arrange to prevent repetition of the unpleasant experience by avoiding this person in the future, making it clear that if necessary he will retaliate, or getting the hostile person locked up in jail or in a mental institution.

The main point is, however, that the calmer one remains in the face of adversity, the more competent he will be in arranging to prevent its recurrence. If a person gets extremely upset by headaches, he sometimes actually avoids seeing a physician, for fear that he will be told he is afflicted with some dread disease. If he becomes enormously angry at someone who strikes him, he may not avoid that person in the future or have him apprehended, but may actually seek him out, get into a real feud with him, and thus invite future blows. Even well-defined physical ills, therefore, are likely to become aggravated instead of ameliorated if one reacts to them in highly emotional, illogical ways.

Two interesting variations on the theme of meeting adversities with rational attitudes are the what-difference-does-it-really-make and the ten-years-from-now approaches. Using the first of these approaches, a person who finds himself becoming unduly upset over a neurotic's behavior can ask himself: "What difference does it really make? Because of Jim's neurosis, he's saying nasty things to me. Do they *really* hurt? Or do they hurt just because I am *letting* them hurt? Will he stop loving me because he's saying those things? Will I drop dead of a heart attack if I hear him say them? Will my boss fire me in the morning because of them? Of course not! Why, then, should I get so excited about what he is saying? Why give it an importance it really doesn't have?"

Using the ten-years-from-now variation, a person would say to himself: "Those certainly are terrible things Jim is saying about me. But what's the very worst that can happen because of what Jim says? Perhaps he will no longer like me; or he may turn others against me, or I might lose my job because of his statements. Will it really spoil my whole life if any of these things actually happen? And even if I am unhappy right now, what effect will it all have ten years from now? Will I even remember this incident then? Probably not. So why should I get so excited about it now?"

By using these and similar techniques, one can, as Epictetus demonstrated many centuries ago, use reason to eradicate virtually all kinds of mental or emotional unhappiness. But to employ these rational techniques, one must truly believe in them. Telling oneself that a thing makes no difference now, nor will make any ten years from now, or telling oneself that the behavior of a neurotic friend or relative should not be a source of annoyance, will not work unless one actually *believes* what he is saying. Merely telling oneself is not enough: a person must thoroughly convince himself. And he usually can. For it is a common failing to exaggerate the importance of what one does and of what others do to us. If a person thinks about these things, and objectively assesses what their true importance is, he will not be nearly so disturbed about them.

Questioning the importance of the things that happen can of course itself be taken to illogical extremes. For, though it is true that we are mortal human beings, and that ten or a hundred years from now what has happened today may well be of little or no importance, it is hardly true that what happens today is of *no* significance. If a neurotic associate, for example, hits one on the jaw, the victim will, at the very least, have a sore jaw; and that will be quite important to the injured party, if not to anyone else.

There is no point in telling oneself that *nothing* is important and hence one should never worry about anything. This technique, in fact, is a typical neurotic mechanism, whereby the individual convinces himself that he is of no importance whatever, nor is anything or anyone else, and therefore whatever happens to him does not matter. To a healthy, self-esteeming individual, what happens very definitely *does* matter. But the point is that one should not let it matter *too* much.

As usual, the best solution to the problem is a kind

of Aristotelian mean between two extremes—that is, one should adopt that philosophic attitude which enables him to live between the extremes of under- and over-exaggeration. A person should not, on the one hand, build up the importance of things so that his life seems to depend on their occurring or not occurring, nor should he, on the other hand, convince himself that nothing has any importance whatsoever. One should find significance in whatever things he likes. But if he cannot have what he likes, he must not feel that the world is coming to an end. It is too bad that he cannot have what he prefers, but not necessarily catastrophic.

This is especially true in one's dealings with neurotics. The things they do are often inconvenient, annoying, shocking. There is no use trying to gloss over that fact. But, truly, are they so very bad? Will the world fall completely apart because of these neurotic acts? Or does the "normal" person make neurotic acts appear worse by overemphasizing their bad aspects or exaggerating their importance?

It is worth while to try to stop harping upon and exaggerating the troubles a neurotic causes and to concentrate on the fact that he is sufficiently disturbed to display annoying symptoms, but not on the symptoms themselves. Make every effort to be more philosophic about the annoyances he brings about.

The final, and by far the best, thing one can do in order to live successfully with seriously troubled people is to work for the improvement and stabilization of his own personality structure. Nothing, in fact, is more important than this.

Instructive in this connection is the work of the professional psychotherapist. Recent investigations have tended to show that the main asset of the competent psychologist may not be his training or his experience, but his own personality. It is by the actual use of this personality that he best manages to help others.

By using his own inner resources, the therapist serves as a good model for his patients. He leads them into healthier byways, his own health serving as proof that treading these byways is beneficial. He refuses to enter into sick relationships with them as other, weaker personalities than he have done previously. And he is able to give them strength because he is so little preoccupied with his own problems that he has sufficient time and energy to help them with theirs.

The psychotherapist's personality is an essential part of his therapeutic technique. Without a strong, basically non-neurotic ego-structure, he would tend to fall into the same trap with his patients that their other associates fell into, and would tend to aggravate rather than to help cure their neuroses.

The psychotherapist, moreover, rarely becomes disturbed himself by the antics of his patients, in spite of the abuse he sometimes takes from them. He accepts their name-calling, ingratitude, and blame and refuses to become upset. He can do this partly because, since it is his job, he has become inured to it, but also because he is such a relatively stable, well adjusted, well analyzed individual himself that he can withstand abuse and, in spite of it, be willing and able to help the abuser.

Taking a lesson from the experience of the psychotherapist, one can easily see that, if he would best handle a neurotic, he should look into his own personality and see how it is functioning. The better adjusted he is himself, the more likely he is to be able, with real equanimity, to withstand the annoyances which inevitably arise in relationships with disturbed individuals.

Of course one cannot simply say to himself: "Now look here, old fellow. You've just got to buck up and be non-neurotic yourself if you are to live successfully with neurotics." This, in itself, would be futile. What a person must do is take an inventory of his own neurotic traits and trends, try to understand as much as he possibly can about neurosis in general and himself in particular, and make some attempt to work through his disturbances.

Usually, to do a good job in this respect, one needs some psychotherapeutic help. A person is quite likely to be too close to himself to be objective; he overlooks his own neurotic trends, or, even when he finds them, he is inclined to rationalize or to work through them in a hazy, partial manner. This is not to say that self-analysis is worthless; indeed, it may be extremely valuable. But for a thorough analytic job, one usually needs the help of a well-trained, competent outside observer who will provide assistance and guidance in one's self-explorations, and enable one to see many things about himself of which he is partly or completely unconscious.

It is not merely conscious thinking that tends to make and keep one neurotic, but unconscious thoughts and feelings as well. A person often becomes disturbed because he is ashamed to face certain things (he unconsciously and illogically thinks of them as terrible) and because he erects various unconscious defenses against facing these things. He stays disturbed because he consciously thinks he is trying to help himself, when subconsciously he is maintaining the same irrational beliefs that originally caused his self-defeating behavior.

The unconscious thinking and feeling processes—which serve as both the original sources of, and the main perpetuating factors in, emotional disturbance —are difficult to get at by oneself. If they were not, no one would develop neurotic symptoms. But with the help of a trained psychotherapist or analyst, it is usually not too difficult to get at unconscious thinking and feeling and to understand oneself more fully. Neurotic trends can then be unraveled and worked through; and one's insight into others may be increased remarkably.

Therefore, if a person has serious neurotic tendencies, he should make a sincere effort to understand and overcome them. If he can, unaided, truly resolve and cope with these tendencies, well and good. If he cannot, then he should honestly admit he is having difficulties and seek competent psychotherapeutic aid. No matter how time-consuming and expensive such aid may at first appear to be, not to obtain it will, in the long run, be infinitely more costly, both to oneself and to any deeply disturbed friend or relative he may wish to help.

A final word: Neurotics, in our culture, are tragically abundant. And this sad situation exists largely because we insist that human beings be champions, successes, and millionaires on the one hand, and angels, demigods, and saints on the other. But one can't have saintliness and have to fight like the devil to get it. And when one is *blamed* for not being able to be both a saint and a championship fighter to the nth degree of perfection, neurosis is certain to abound.

Consequently, as long as we live in our society, we will inevitably meet seriously troubled people. As we do, we must always remember these things: neurotics are neurotic; they are not to blame for being troubled; they became neurotic because they adopted irrational beliefs that led to deep-seated feelings of inadequacy and hostility; and they will become more disturbed if we make no allowances for their difficulties.

If *you* find it impossible to learn and apply these fundamental facts about human neurosis, then you should in all honesty be suspicious of your own serious neurotic trends. If you can learn, as most probably you can, to apply these facts, you are almost certain to do yourself and others inestimable benefit.

Will you accept this great challenge?

SELECTED READINGS

SELECTED READINGS

All contemporary writing in the field of personality theory, clinical psychology, psychoanalysis, and psychiatry is to be taken with many reservations. These areas are still in their infancy as far as scientific, verified knowledge is concerned, and there is much that we are learning about them almost every day.

The fields of psychoanalysis and personality theory, moreover, are overrun with many schools and theorists, all of whom tend to believe that they know exactly what makes human beings neurotic and what may be done about curing them. Unfortunately, however, these schools and theorists, especially the most orthodox of them, rarely agree on many important questions, and directly contradict most of the other writers in the field.

The intelligent reader, therefore, will take modern psychological writings with due skepticism, and will consider many of them little more than brilliant hypotheses which have yet to be factually proved or disproved. Nonetheless, for anyone who is to understand himself and others, some amount of reading in the field of modern dynamic psychology is essential.

With this in mind, and with the fervent hope that the reader will take all psychological theories with sufficient grains of salt, and will think for himself and apply these theories to his own experience before he religiously adheres to any, the following list of selected readings is offered.

ADLER, ALFRED. *Understanding Human Nature*. New York: Greenberg, 1927.

ALEXANDER, FRANZ, and FRENCH, THOMAS M. *Psychoanalytic Therapy*. New York: Ronald Press, 1946.

ANSBACHER, HEINZ, and ANSBACHER, ROWENA. *The Individual Psychology of Alfred Adler*. New York: Basic Books, 1956.

CAMERON, NORMAN, and MAGARET, ANN. *Behavior Pathology*. Boston: Houghton Mifflin, 1951.

DOLLARD, JOHN, and MILLER, NEAL E. *Personality and Psychotherapy*. New York: McGraw-Hill, 1950.

ELLIS, ALBERT. *The American Sexual Tragedy*. New York: Twayne Publishers, 1954.

———. *An Introduction to the Scientific Principles of Psychoanalysis*. Provincetown, Mass.: The Journal Press, 1950.

———. "New Approaches to Psychotherapy Techniques." Brandon, Vermont: *Journal of Clinical Psychology*, 1955.

———. "Outcome of Employing Three Techniques of Psychotherapy." *ibid.*, October, 1957, Volume 13, No. 4.

FENICHEL, OTTO. *Psychoanalytic Theory of Neurosis.* **New** York: Norton, 1945.

FREEMAN, LUCY. *Fight Against Fears.* New York: Crown, 1951.

FREUD, SIGMUND. *Basic Writings.* New York: Modern Library, 1938.

———. *An Outline of Psychoanalysis.* New York: Norton, 1949.

FROMM, ERICH. *Man for Himself.* New York: Rinehart, 1947.

———. *The Sane Society.* New York: Rinehart, 1955.

FROMM-REICHMANN, FRIEDA. *Principles of Intensive Psychotherapy.* Chicago: University of Chicago Press, 1950.

JONES, ERNEST. *The Life and Works of Sigmund Freud.* 3 vols. New York: Basic Books, 1955-57.

HORNEY, KAREN. *The Neurotic Personality of Our Time.* New York: Norton, 1937.

———. *New Ways in Psychoanalysis.* New York: Norton, 1939.

JUNG, C. G. *The Practice of Psychotherapy.* New York: Pantheon, 1954.

KELLY, GEORGE A. *The Psychology of Personal Constructs.* New York: Norton, 1955.

KNIGHT, JOHN. *The Story of My Psychoanalysis.* New York: Pocket Books, 1952.

KRAINES, S. H., and THETFORD, E. S. *Managing Your Mind.* New York, Macmillan, 1947.

McCARY, JAMES L., and SCHEER, DANIEL E. (eds.) *Six Approaches to Psychotherapy.* New York: Dryden Press, 1955.

MASLOW, A. H. *Motivation and Personality.* New York: Harper, 1954.

MAY, ROLLO. *Man's Search for Himself.* New York: Norton, 1953.

MULLAHY, PATRICK. *Oedipus, Myth and Complex.* New York: Hermitage Press, 1948.

MUNROE, RUTH L. *Schools for Psychoanalytic Thought.* New York: Dryden Press, 1955.

PENNINGTON, L. A., and BERG, IRWIN A. (eds.) *An Introduction to Clinical Psychology*. New York: Ronald Press, 2d ed., 1954.

RIESMAN, DAVID, and others. *The Lonely Crowd*. New York: Doubleday Anchor Books, 1953.

ROGERS, CARL R. *Client-Centered Therapy*. Boston: Houghton Mifflin, 1951.

SAPPENFIELD, BERT R. *Personality Dynamics*. New York: Knopf, 1954.

SILVERBERG, WILLIAM V. *Childhood Experience and Personal Destiny*. New York: Springer, 1952.

SULLIVAN, HARRY STACK. *The Interpersonal Theory of Psychiatry*. New York: Norton, 1953.

THOMPSON, CLARA. *Psychoanalysis: Evolution and Development*. New York: Hermitage, 1950.

THORNE, FREDERIC C. "Principles of Personality Counseling." Brandon, Vermont: *Journal of Clinical Psychology*, 1950.

WOLBERG, LEWIS R. *The Technique of Psychotherapy*. New York: Grune & Stratton, 1954.